Homilies for the **Whole Community**

Wisdom from a Pastor's Heart

YEAR B

REVEREND MICHAEL T. HAYES

Kathleen M. Groh, General Editor

TWENTY
THIRD *23rd*
PUBLICATIONS

Twenty-Third Publications
A Division of Bayard
One Montauk Avenue, Suite 200
New London, CT 06320
(860) 437-3012 or (800) 321-0411
www.twentythirdpublications.com
ISBN:1-58595-534-5

The Scripture passages contained herein are from the *New Revised Standard Version of the Bible*, copyright ©1989, by the Division of Christian Education of the National Council of Churches in the U.S.A. All rights reserved.

The Celtic art used on the divider pages represents a lion, the symbol for the evangelist Mark, whose gospel is read during Year B.

Library of Congress Catalog Card Number: 2005929697
Printed in the U.S.A.

Contents

Ordinary Time

Other Feasts & Occasions

Fr. Michael T. Hayes

Michael T. Hayes was born in Lahinch, Co. Clare, Ireland. As he liked to say, he was "the only child (unspoiled) of Margaret and Michael Hayes." He spent his youth on Ireland's west coast beaches and as a caddy at the world-famous Lahinch National Golf Course. The love of the game never left him. The family later moved to Brosna and he attended high school at St. Flannan's in Ennis, Ireland.

After earning top scholastic honors and completing seminary at St. Patrick's, Carlow, Ireland, he was ordained for the Diocese of Duluth on June 10, 1960, where he served in parish ministry for forty-three years. He claimed "Life, Be in It" as his motto and became well-known for his non-judgmental approach to ministry, his sense of humor, and his generosity.

Fr. Mike was a gifted storyteller and a lover of literature, poetry, theater, and music. Irish culture permeated his ministry. Fr. Hayes was the founder and pastor of Holy Angels Catholic Church in Moose Lake, Minnesota, and served this community for seventeen years. After a brief, courageous struggle with cancer, parishioners and friends from all walks of life celebrated the life and death of this perfectly outrageous, witty, and wise shepherd on August 11, 2003.

Foreword

Is there anything more important in the church than good liturgy? The liturgies of Word and Eucharist, the Liturgy of the Hours, the rites of the various other sacraments and rites of the church are our life blood. We don't just celebrate the Eucharist; we are the Eucharist! And in our liturgies, the "breaking open of the Word" done by our homilists is also very important. For most Catholic people, this is their one and only catechetical moment of the week. For many who attend infrequently, it might be their moment for the month, or for the year.

This collection of homilies is a very important piece in the unfolding drama of whole community catechesis in the Church today. In whole community catechesis, we see every element of parish life as catechizing. How we behave and what we say in public tells more than textbooks or lectures ever could!

I never knew Fr. Michael Hayes, but after reading this collection, I almost feel like I do know him now. I can just see him, sitting there in his booth at the local diner, reflecting and talking and drinking coffee as the church came and went each week. I'm glad these are being shared with you and I hope they will help you bring the Word alive each week.

I'm reminded of that old tale about a small town where there lived a wise old woman. People came from all the surrounding countryside to seek her advice and accept her wisdom. But two youngsters in that town thought better. They didn't believe she was really wise. So they concocted a plan to fool the old woman. They decided to go to her, with a tiny bird cupped in their hands. They planned to ask her whether the bird was alive or dead. If she said it was alive, they would crush it and show her that it was dead. If she said it was dead, they'd release it and show her that it was alive. "She's not so smart," they said to themselves, "at least not as smart as we are!"

So they went to her one day, a tiny bird cupped in their hands. "Old woman," they asked, "is this bird alive—or is it dead?"

She looked them straight in the eye, paused, and then said, "Well, I guess the answer to that is in your hands, isn't it?"

As a homilist, you have a lot in your hands, too. Sharing Fr. Hayes's wisdom here is a real gift. Thanks for what you do each week as our wisdom figure, the one who breaks open the Word for us. Thanks for the work you put into this and the love with which you deliver it to us. And thanks for being open to the wisdom of this wise man from Moose Lake, Minnesota.

—Bill Huebsch

holey, Wholly, holy

We had just finished thoroughly cleaning the old rectory at St. Francis in Carlton, Minnesota, on a hot summer afternoon. Our pastor was leaving and we were anticipating his short-term replacement. As we were sipping sodas, we heard voices coming through the back door.

Fr. Joe Hughes walked in, and following shyly behind him was a tall, slightly slouching young priest with rumpled clothes. After introductions, he asked in a deep, Irish brogue what everyone did for the parish. I was in a bit of a panic because everyone else had official titles like president of the rosary society, secretary, housekeeper, and then he came to me. I simply said, "I'm the minister of hospitality!" Fr. Michael Hayes' blue eyes lit up in delight.

I must admit that I had no idea what "minister of hospitality" would mean in his life or mine when I took on the position, but I thought my first role was to "unrumple" him, so I offered to do his laundry. He basically had a few golf clothes, one black shirt, and a suit that he "borrowed" from Bishop William Casey of Paterson, New Jersey. He would say that he had "anticipated the bishop's generosity."

I soon found that his cigarette smoking was going to be his nemesis. He had holes from cigarette burns in everything he owned, from his car seats, golf shirts, and sweaters, to his polyester pants. An ugly, blue herringboned pair of pants was particularly "holey." During one of the washings, I just hung them on the line and figured that if he didn't get those wretched things back, he wouldn't even miss them. He never said a thing.

Toward the end of the summer, a good friend and co-parishioner asked me if I wanted to put anything in her garage sale, so I scooped up the pants and thought, "Good riddance." That afternoon, I heard a car door slam in the driveway and looked out. There, on the drive stood the pastor of St. Francis, wearing none other than the "holey pants" that he claimed he found in the thrift store!

Goodness knows I wasn't the only woman in his many parishes that tried to make Fr. Mike a bit more presentable. Even when his clothes were cleaned and perfectly pressed, he could look unmatched and wrinkled in five minutes. He once remarked that "If someone has to recognize that I am a priest by the clothes I wear, I'm not a very good one."

"Wholly" described Fr. Mike's ministry. It was inclusive of everyone, from the prisoners in the Moose Lake Correctional Facility to the elderly in the nursing homes of Carlton and Moose Lake, Minnesota. His ministry extended from the very famous to the traveler who slipped off the freeway looking for a handout and gas money.

He was wholly present to all of his parishioners, young and old, even the ones he had left behind when he moved on to a new parish. He never stopped being our pastor, because he entered our lives deeply and sincerely, bringing the presence of Christ in words and actions.

Fr. Mike was with us in our happiest times, whether it was in a local restaurant, gala events at the church, or in the Knappogue Castle in Ireland. He was there for great food and good company. Be it baptisms, first communions, confirmations, or weddings, he brought with him his profound thoughts and prayers and sprinkled them with humor for good measure.

Our most heartfelt times came when we struggled with grief and pain from sickness or the death of spouses, children, parents, and grandparents. His liturgies were carefully chosen, written and delivered with gentle compassion, but with firm conviction in the resurrection. Not only that, he remained long after the crowds left, even if it was only to make a quick phone call at just the right moment, to let someone know that they were being thought of.

The last word, "holy" means "coming from God." We were blessed by God with Fr. Mike's gifted presence among us. With his great love of literature, he took delight in creatively and skillfully playing with words and ideas. His weekly homilies were close to pure poetry. He never once complained that he had to get ready for Sunday. Instead, he would sit in his favorite diner booth late into Friday evening until he had a fresh and challenging homily for his community. He would then call me, many times after 11:00 PM to say that he had "nailed it."

By the time I moved to the Twin Cities in 1988, I was a long-time parishioner and friend of Fr. Mike. Soon after, he began to send me his homilies. Every Wednesday, the envelope would arrive, stuffed not only with the hand-written homily, but with newspaper clippings, jokes, Irish publications, and anything else he would find in his briefcase. I stored them in boxes that soon began to stack up. I would take some of the homilies to my office and use them for presentations on Eucharist and reconciliation. Many of the homilies were shared with fellow staff members for Bible study and Rite of Christian Initiation of Adults. For thirteen years, I collected these homilies.

After Fr. Mike's death in August 2003, I spent the next lenten season putting the homilies in notebooks. One morning I e-mailed Bill Huebsch and asked him if he had any ideas about publishing them. His response was "Send me one." The return e-mail read: "They are poetry!" Soon after, we met for lunch and a great adventure began.

With Bill's encouragement, the consent of Fr. Mike's cousins, and the help of faithful and talented friends, I have chosen sixty-four homilies for Year B that illustrate the heart and mind of a truly holy man.

The homilies have been re-created in style and color. Fr. Mike wrote them to be proclaimed, so the movement of the words and the emphasis of the words could be seen as he preached. Use them as you see fit; they can be imitated or emulated. Sprinkled among them are anecdotes and stories from his many friends to give you another glimpse into the life of this unique priest.

I hope you enjoy and are moved by these treasured homilies as you read and ponder them. But it is my greatest desire that you find places to use these homilies, in part or totally, and proclaim them in your ministry to the whole community.

This collection of homilies is lovingly dedicated to

Mary Colleen

Beautiful, talented

Dancing-black eyes

Loving wife and mother

Daughter

—Kathleen M. Groh

Advent & Christmas

Isa 63:16b–17, 19b, 64:2–7; 1 Cor 1:3–9; Mk 13:33–37

Presence in the Present

"Therefore, keep awake—
   for you do not know when the master of the house will come,
   in the evening,
   or at midnight,
   or at cockcrow,
   or at dawn...." (Mark 13:35)

The Gospel of Mark is telling us to
   watch.
Is this a reference to the Second Coming?
   Yes.
Could it also mean the moment when death intrudes
   and Christ comes?
   Yes
Could it also refer to the graced moment
   when God in our neighbor, or nature, or art
   is suddenly present to us?
   Yes.
There is indeed an apocalyptic element to our faith.
But it is not to be understood
   that the Lord was hiding away for several centuries
   and then returning at a time we least expect,
      just to catch us in a bad light.

In Shakespeare's play *Measure for Measure*
   we have an example of just that.
In the play, the king goes undercover in his own kingdom
   in order to observe his subjects at work.
While disguised he specifically asks people
   what they think of the absent king.

He finds several less than edifying things that they think about him
    and that they do in his absence.

Though indeed, there will be an unexpected nature
    to Jesus' Second Coming,
    it is not his intention
        to catch us derelict in our duties.
Neither is it the intention of Jesus,
    at the moment of our own death
        to catch us derelict in our duties.
And then there is the Lord's coming in each moment.
Karl Rahner, noted theologian, called it
        "the inbreaking of the Lord's presence in the present."
These are words we should remember everyday,

"Truly I tell you, just as you did it to one of the least of these
    who are members of my family,
    you did it to me." (Matthew 25:40)

On the First Sunday of Advent the liturgy is about
    staying awake,
    keeping alert,
        anticipating the coming of Christ in our daily lives.

Think of those early followers who reacted to his return
    after he had been away.
Remember when he came to the home of Mary and Martha?
Someone told Martha he was on his way.
She couldn't wait
    and she went down the road to meet him.
Mary was at home.
When she heard that he was there,
she leaped up from where she was seated,
    and hurried into his presence.
Her only regret was that he hadn't come sooner!

This was how his first friends reacted to his coming.
How can we think of it as something to dread, or fear?!
Has he changed?
    No.
Jesus Christ, the same yesterday, today, and forever.
Are we that much different from them?
    No.
We are people just like them.
It was just that they had found a faithful friend
    who had taught them the meaning of love and forgiveness.
When we learn that,
    we will see his coming as a promise and not a threat.

Jesus said, "Beware, keep alert,
    for you do not know when the time will come." (Mark 13:33)
We can hear this as a warning
    lest Christ should come and catch us in some kind of mischief.
Or we can hear it as a wake-up call,
    lest Christ should come and we do not even know it.
Wouldn't it be ironic,
    if we were waiting for him to appear in the sky
        and he should walk right past us?

It is true that the Lord has promised to return at the end of time.
But there is no reason for us to wait
    and wonder about some future date.
We can take Advent, his coming seriously, today.
Even better, be Advent to others.
If you do, no one will have to wish you
    a merry, joyful, and blessed Christmas.
You will already be experiencing
    the graced moments of this blessed season.

May your presents this Christmas
    be the gift of time together—
        the gift of presence.

Isa 40:1–5, 9–11; 2 Pet 3, 8–14; Mk 1:1–8

Two Warriors

What a powerful man John the Baptist must have been!
Here he is dressed in camel's hair and a leather belt,
    munching on grasshoppers,
    and staring down wild bees for their honey
        like some great black bear.
No wonder people went out to see him near the Jordan.
Can't you see the travel posters?
    Ride the baptizer water slide!
    See the wild man take on a brood of vipers!

In Advent we usually think of Mary as the star of our church pageant,
    with the child Jesus waiting in the wings.
But two strong, grown-up males
    are key supporting cast members:
    the prophets Isaiah and John the Baptist.
Both are interesting men.
In the language of the men's movement,
    these prophets are "warriors."
By definition, warriors are people
    who protect the children and the earth.
They do not shame others and do not allow shame.
Women as well as men can be warriors.
These warriors are nonviolent.
They protect us from shame,
    but unlike savages, they do not hurt the innocent.
Isaiah and John are warriors for God's Word.
They go before the Lord
    clearing paths,
    crying out,
    protecting the innocent from those trying to hurt them.

The innocent are to be protected from hurt and shame.
We need to hear this message in
　　our churches, our families, and our neighborhoods.
Too often, churches have stood by
　　while innocents are hurt in families.
Or worse, they have defended the violent parent
　　under the guise of parental authority.
Besides being cruel, this is lousy theology.
Batterers and the people they abuse
　　sometimes use scriptural passages to justify their behaviors.
True, in ancient biblical times, men owned their wives and children
　　　and could even sell them into slavery.
We know now that this is sinful.
Jesus treated women as equals;
　　perhaps his mother had something to do with that.

A healthy and holy family relationship
　　is a powerful and even divine human experience.
But the power in families must be used wisely.
Abusive power over someone lesser, smaller, and weaker
　　is a violent kind of power.
It is unholy.
The power found in loving families gives children
　　a sense of their own worth.
It gives them hope and confidence that they can do wonders,
　　and that they have limitless possibilities.

Children *do* have that kind of a future.
It is we, the adults, that feel stunted and hemmed in by our choices.
Think of the different ways children and adults feel about
　　the approaching Christmas feast.
Kids feel that always, anything can happen.
Some adults feel they are lucky if anything good happens.

Today's reading from 2 Peter comes down on the side of children,
　　and favors the childlike approach to faith.

"In accordance with his promise,
 we wait for new heavens and a new earth,
 where righteousness is at home." (2 Peter 3:13)
So how can we be the powerful prophets of God's Word,
 creating a new earth where God's righteousness is at home?
Start in your own home.
Treat your spouse, parents, and children
 with the respect and dignity they deserve.
Honor your wives; honor your husbands.
Discipline children out of love, not out of anger.
Any other way is abusive and can leave a lifetime of scars.

Isaiah and John were forerunners of Jesus, strong and powerful men,
 who knew that someone greater was to come,
 someone they could follow and admire.
They worked all their lives
 for what they believed and hoped would come to be;
  the reign of God on earth,
  a place of justice and mercy,
  of kindness and truth,
  a place of love.
Our Advent journey follows the same path.
We walk in their sandal prints.

At this liturgy, let us make an act of communion
 with all the victims of abusive power.
Include the victim born in a stable,
 and raised on a cross.
Let us honor our Christ and all victims
 by filling ourselves with the bread of life
 and then toast one another with the cup of salvation.

A Glimpse of Fr. Hayes

Robert Bly, author of "Iron John," had a summer home in Moose Lake. He would often be seen having coffee and deep conversations with Fr. Mike in a booth at the local diner. These "warriors" enjoyed their literary relationship.

Isa 61:1–2a, 10–11; 1 Thess 5:16–24; Jn 1:6–8, 19–28

Popeye Had It Right!

"I am five-fold blest.…If I were anyone else, I would envy me."

— Leonard Bernstein

There are a lot of people in this world
    who never have figured out who they are,
    and there are many others
    who, if they ever knew, have forgotten.

In the gospel today, a group of people
    came to John the Baptist and asked him this direct question,
        "Who are you?" (John 1:19)
He could have simply replied,
    "I am John, the son of Zechariah."
But that was not how John answered
    because that was not what they were asking.
They really wanted to know how he saw himself
    and what he regarded as his role in life.
John answered,
    "I am the voice of one crying out in the wilderness.
    Make straight the way of the Lord." (John 1:23)
What a beautiful way for John to identify himself.
He wasn't just mind and body.
He wasn't even just spirit.
He was purpose.
God had called him because there was something for him to do
    and he was doing it.

It reminds me of Popeye, the sailor man,
    who so often said,
    "I am who I am."

"Who are you?"
How would you and I answer this question?
Just name alone is not enough.
We have to go beyond that,
    or else we will never really understand who we are.

John was the most famous man of his time,
    and it is not surprising that he held a high opinion of himself.
His fame had nothing to do with his self respect;
    that came from other sources
    all of which are available to ordinary people like you and me.
Public opinion tried to make John
    into somebody other than who he was.
Some thought he was the Messiah.
Others thought he was Elijah.
Still others thought he was the prophet foretold in Deuteronomy.

But John disowned all these titles and went on being himself.
He was a strange man, a kind of social misfit.
He lived in the wilderness
    and he wore strange clothes and ate strange foods.
(He munched on grasshoppers before he knew about salsa!)
But for John that was good enough.
He accepted himself for who he was.
We can never hold a high opinion of ourselves
    by pretending to be someone else.
That is make-believe, a game children play.
When adults play that game, it is called insanity.

You and I do not need to be anyone
    other than who we are.
We many not seem like much
    but we are who we are.
That is reality,
    and it is much better than any kind of pretense.
This kind of acceptance is possible for all of us.

Accept yourself for who you are, and do not try to be anyone else.
We can all do that.
John was called "a man sent from God!"
The same title applies to you and me.
Every one of us
     is a man or woman sent from God.
We are not accidents of nature.

John was conceived and born when his father was an old man
     and his mother was past the age of childbearing.
It was a miracle.
Our birth may have been quite ordinary
     but that does not matter.
A thing does not have to be unusual for God to be involved in it.
Every day we live with miracles that we fail to see
     simply because we have gotten used to them.
Every human life, including yours and mine,
     is a miracle of God.

Allow me to suggest that you do a little editing of the Bible.
The passage is John 1:6.
Take a pen, cross out "John,"
     and write in your own name.
If you are female, cross out the word "man"
     and write in the word "woman."
The verse will then read:
"There was a man named Joe sent by God,"
     or "There was a woman named Helen sent by God."
That verse will be no less true then
     than it is now.
Your life has a divine origin.
It is too sacred to be wasted.
If we get the picture clearly in our minds,
     it will be increasingly difficult for us
     to violate life's sanctities.
John was an advance man for Advent.
His mission was to prepare the people for the coming of Christ.

The good news is that you and I can do the same thing
   by the words we speak,
   by the deeds we do,
   by the attitudes we show.
We can help make the world
   a little more receptive to the coming of Christ.

The Third Sunday of Advent used to be called Gaudete Sunday
   from the Latin word "rejoice."
Let us rejoice in who we are!
Popeye had it right!
   "I am who I am," said Popeye the sailor man.

2 Sam 7:1–5, 8b–12,14a; Rom 16:25–27; Lk 1:26–38

What Are We Going to Give God?

The family was making a list of the people they wanted to remember
    with a Christmas gift.
The list was almost complete
    when the four-year-old daughter asked,
    "What are we going to give God?"

The older children giggled,
    while mother and father suppressed a smile.
But to her, the question was quite logical.
She had been told that God had given us
    this wonderful world,
    and that God had given us life, food, clothing,
        and the baby Jesus.
It was only natural for her to ask,
    "What are we going to give God?"

Children have a way of raising
    the most profound theological questions.
The whole story of religion lies in back of that little girl's question.
From ancient altars stained with blood,
    to modern offering plates filled with money,
    people have been wondering what to give God.
We do not know how the family answered the little girl.
How would you have answered her?
What could we possibly give to God,
    the creator of all things?
What would be a suitable gift?

It is another version of that old question,
 "What do you give the person who already has everything?!"
Maybe we can shed some light on this subject
 by recalling the kinds of giving that takes place among us.
The presents we give and receive vary widely,
 not simply in monetary value,
 but also in moral quality.
Some of our gifts are so selfish
 that they hardly deserve the name.
They are given for the express purpose
 of gaining favorable consideration for ourselves.
For example, a businessman makes a generous gift or donation
 to someone running for public office.
That can be acceptable, even commendable.
The man may simply be participating in the political process.
He may consider his donation an investment
 in the future of the community
 or he may be trying to influence legislation
 that will benefit him and his business.

In the latter case, his donation is at least unethical
 and perhaps even illegal.
We have invented an ugly word to describe this kind of gift.
It is called a bribe.
Surely, we understand that this kind of gift is unacceptable to God.
We cannot *do* or *give* anything
 that will *obligate* God to us.
If that is the motivation of our giving,
 we would be better off not to give at all.
At least we will not be putting God
 on the level of a corrupt politician.
Can anything be more silly
 than the thought that God can be bribed?

There is another kind of gift, a better gift,
    that grows out of a sense of obligation.
Some people are on our Christmas lists
    simply because they ought to be.
We owe it to them.
To leave them off would be unthinkable.
We are glad to give them a present.
We are not trying to flatter or influence these people.
It is only right and decent to give them a present.

That same principle applies in our giving to God.
There is an element of obligation involved.
God has given us life,
    and God has the right to expect
    that we do something good and decent with this priceless gift.
The prophet Micah said it like this:
    "With what shall I come before the Lord?" (Micah 6:6)
And God answers,
"He has told you, O mortal, what is good;
    and what does the Lord require of you
        but to do justice,
        and to love kindness,
        and to walk humbly with your God?" (Micah 6:8)

Micah says the Lord *requires* this of us.
In other words, we owe it to him
    to be fair in all our dealings,
    to treat people with kindness and consideration and
    not to be the least bit proud for having done it.
We are duty-bound to present God
    with the gift of a decent and honorable life.

But, there is something better than a duty gift.
That is a love gift.
The value of a love gift is,
    not in what it costs (it could be a child's drawing)
    but in what it means or symbolizes.

A love gift represents the very heart and soul of the giver.
We read of such a gift in today's gospel.
The angel told Mary that she was God's chosen instrument,
    through whom God would give his Son to the world.
The next move was up to Mary, and here is her response:
"Here am I, the servant of the Lord;
    let it be with me according to your word." (Luke 1:38)
Mary gave herself,
    and that is the best gift possible.

The little girl wanted to know
    "What are we going to give God?"

The mature answer is written in the last verse of Isaac Watts' great hymn
"When I Survey the Wondrous Cross." It says,

"Were the whole realm of nature mine,
    that were a present far too small.
Love so amazing, so divine,
    demands my soul, my life, my all."

This is the gift God really wants from you and me.

This year, why not give the best gift of all to God:
    yourself.
You can give this same gift
    to the people you love,
    and to the people who need your love.
In the words of a Danish proverb:
    "He who gives to me, teaches me to give."

A Glimpse of Fr. Hayes

A few years ago, Advent ended on Sunday. This gave us only the few hours of Monday to change from quiet purples to a celebration of white and gold.

And so, early Monday morning, down came the draping behind the altar; in came the freshly cut tree, donated each year by a family who grows Christmas trees as a sideline. Soon, little white lights and gold ribbon were wrapped throughout its branches. Father liked the decorations to be fairly clean. He wanted the emphasis on our little crèche, which we snuggled in front of the altar, surrounded by a cloud of poinsettias. We stood back and surveyed our work, looked at our watches and declared it good.

I scurried to the grocery store to pick up last minute items I would need when our family gathered around our own tree at home tomorrow morning. I was sweating from all the physical work and the stress of the timeline, and I allowed myself the uncharitable thought that Father had no idea what contortions those who decorated the church put ourselves through to see to it that our church was made ready for the Christ Child. All he had to do was show up, put on his fancy white vestments, and celebrate Mass with us.

The Mass! Oh, my goodness! We had moved the side table and candles to make room for the white and gold draping and the tree. The cruets and chalice and the linens and all of it was probably sitting in a pew somewhere, safely protected from all the rushing around. I couldn't remember if anyone had thought to replace them before we left the church.

I threw the rest of my things into my cart, tried to maintain control of my heart rate through the long checkout line, turned into the traffic, and sped back to the church. It had begun to snow, so that even though it was three in the afternoon, cars had their headlights on.

I noticed that there was one set of tire tracks in the fresh inch of snow on the drive. I pulled up to park under the canopy near the church, and noticed Father's car, idling with its lights on, the door not completely closed. I could see his cigarettes stubbed out in the ashtray, his ever-present briefcase open on the seat, the articles from the Irish Times sticking out from under business letters from the diocese, topped by his dog-eared appointment calendar.

I walked up to the main doors, found them locked, and was fumbling with my keys when I heard the inner doors open and saw Father coming toward me. He had not heard me, and we startled each other.

"Father," I exclaimed, "I just remembered we had to set up the altar things. We forgot to move them back. I'll take care of it right now." I couldn't resist adding, "I didn't expect to find you here so early!" Father Hayes had the Irish sense of time, and could always be counted on to be anywhere from four to seven minutes late for anything. The comment was not lost on him, and he gave me the look that said so.

It was just then I noticed that Father was not alone. Tucked under his right arm was not the bundle of papers or forgotten sweater I had assumed it must be, but Holmes, his cat, hanging there as calm as you please, blinking his golden green eyes at me.

I looked from Holmes to Father, speechless. Father said to me, "Ah, yes, Cindy, I knew the church would be ready and I wanted to show it to Holmes before the throng arrived. He approves!" He looked down at his lazy companion and scratched him under his elegant chin. "Well, I'd best be getting on. Wouldn't want to be late." And with that he tucked Holmes gently into his little travel crate, which always occupied the back seat of Father's car, climbed behind the wheel, grabbed a cigarette, and gave me half a wave as he drove off into the snow.

So, it mattered to him after all, the way the church looked for this feast day. And he was excited enough about it that he brought his dear companion along for the treat. My heart twinged just a little to think of this, for it seemed a lonely thing to bring a cat to see the church because you have no human companion with which to share it.

Two hours later, the candles were lit, the choir began singing Christmas hymns, and the pews filled with families reunited for these few special days. We all sang, "Joy to the world! The Lord is come." Father walked down the aisle in his lovely new white vestments, woven of fine linen with just a few threads of gold. He kissed the altar, then stretched open his arms and said, "Good evening and welcome to this most holy celebration of our Lord's birth."

The love flowed around that space, through the people, and back up to Father on the altar. Then I knew that even if his priesthood was lonely at times, there was enough joy and love to get him—and all of us—through the long and ordinary winter days ahead.

— Jacinta Carlson,
Parishioner of Holy Angels Church, Moose Lake, MN

Isa 62:11–12; Ps 97; Lk 2:15–20

Bethlehem Is Everywhere

Bethlehem is everywhere.
No, Jesus was not born in Belfast or Baghdad.
But neither was he the pale Caucasian kid
    whose image most of us grew up with.

If Christianity is our story
    of how the divine came calling,
    then it's bound to be as diverse as we are,
    as parochial as we are, and
    as nationalistic as we are.
But also it must be as cosmic.
Take Christ out of Christmas
    and December becomes the bleakest
    and most colorless month of the year.
"The hint half-guessed, the gift half-understood." (T. S. Elliot)

To know something is to grasp it,
    to take hold of it,
    to control it,
    to limit it.
The utter vulnerability of God-made-Infant
    in Bethlehem is beyond knowing,
      it is mystery.
The mystery of Christmas,
    "the loving kindness of the heart of God,"
    cannot be grasped by the human mind.
It is something, rather somebody,
    who visits us like the dawn from on high.
We have traces in our language of this way of understanding
    when we speak of something "dawning" on us.

The wonder of Christmas cannot be known, or grasped,
  we can only allow it to "dawn" on us.
It may be more of a "God incident" than a coincidence
  that the first Mass on Christmas morning
  is called "the dawn Mass" or "Mass at dawn."

In the play *Tarry Flynn*,
  Patrick Kavanaugh was talking about
  a Christmas of his childhood when he said it was
  "a prayer like a white rose pinned on the Virgin Mary's blouse."
Peter Kavanaugh, his brother, described it as
  "the luxury of a child's soul, like the dawn from on high."

Christmas itself is the greatest present.
There's always a danger that we'll treat Jesus Christ
  as a Christmas visitor,
  delighted to see him come,
  especially when he arrives as a child,
  a baby we don't have to feed, or change, or get up to look after.
No post-natal complication,
  just the comforting glow of the crib,
  the understanding reassurance
  that God has become one of us in Jesus Christ:
  God-made-Infant.
The tremendous feeling of the closeness
  of the Father through the Son.

But visitors, no matter how welcome,
  begin to grate on us after a while.
Nice to meet of course, if only once a year,
  but nicer still to see them off
  and to get back to what we left before the festive break.
If only we could drive him or her to the bus or plane
  and wave them out of our lives
  once we've had our festive high.
If only they would let us back to what we were doing
  before they came.

Not because we love them less,
  but because we love our routines more.

How about Jesus?
He is no visitor at all.
He didn't come with just the one change of clothes.
Not for the weekend, charming us for awhile,
  but for life,
    for all time.
When he became one of us
  God-made-Infant,
  he came to stay.
He did that not to give us a rest from our routines,
  like ordinary visitors do,
  but to change our routines—for good.

Jesus Christ came into my life
  not to take life away,
  but that I might enjoy a new and better life
  and have it to the full.
He wants me to be more fulfilled.
He wants me to be free from guilt, selfishness, and loneliness.

If I can look squarely at my life, my routine,
  my way of doing things
  and if I'm happy with it,
  then I probably don't need Jesus Christ yet—
  apart from the days of December, that is.
But if I'm like most people,
  I'm really wondering where my routine is pushing me.
Caught in the middle of the information highway,
  I can't help wondering
  what is going to run me down next.

Pausing for one of these more quiet moments,
  I feel the weight of guilt for things said and done
  for which I've yet to seek forgiveness.

Looking into my heart,
    I find a barren selfishness which excludes everyone—
        except those who are useful to me.
If I'm happy with the routine, that's fine.
But if I'm hungry for something more,
    then this Christmas
    Jesus Christ has something to say to me.

Go Raibh dochas, siochaim agus gra agat gach iule la. (Gaelic)
    May hope, peace, and love fill you always.

Gen 15:1–6, 21:1–3; Col 3:12–21; Lk 2:22–40

The School of Love

Recent political agendas involve
    a lot of discussion about family values.
Not surprisingly, the political parties differ
    over which family values are the most important.
Opinions vary widely on topics such as
    social welfare, school prayer, and private behavior.
But what does Scripture say about the qualities of a family?
Today, we are invited to reflect
    on what is at the heart of the Christmas celebration: the family.
Even those who belong to no church
    celebrate Christmas as a family festival.
Everyone that can be home, comes home—
    even if it is only for a day.

We talk about the Christian family.
What sets it apart from other families
    that do not belong to the Christian community?
The family is at the service
    of love and life.
It is the school of love where we learn
    the basics of life.
This is where we ourselves are loved
    and taught to love and care for those around us.

We are reminded that the family is also
    at the service of society.
Indeed, it is only when the family is under strain and threat
    that we come to appreciate the close link
    that exists between a wholesome society
        and a healthy family life.

So then what makes the difference between the Christian family
    and those who do not belong to a community of faith?
One way to see this is that
    the Christian family is the Church in miniature.

In today's reading from Colossians,
    Paul gives two set of instructions.
We can read it as instructions to the Church in general,
    but also as instructions to the families that make up this Church.
Let's take what Paul says of the Church
    and think of it as the qualities of a real family
    sitting in the pews here today.
"As God's chosen ones, holy and beloved, clothe yourselves
    with compassion, kindness, humility, meekness, and patience.
Forgive each other just as the Lord has forgiven you." (Col 3:12–13)
This means that your family is meant to be
    a place of worship and prayer
    where parents and children recognize
    their dependence on God and each other.
Your prayers don't have to be elaborate.
Simple things like mealtime prayers
    and prayers at bedtime, when the joys and sorrows of the day
        are put to rest.
A simple blessing and wish for success
    as family members leave and enter your home.
The Christian family is meant to be
    a place where faith in Jesus Christ
    is naturally handed on and nurtured daily.
All the lovely textbooks and work of catechists can only compliment,
    not make up for, the work of the parents.
The Christian family is meant to be a haven,
    and a refuge for others in what can sometimes be
        a hard and heartless world.

Do you remember Richard Jewell?
He was the man who was investigated for the bombings in Atlanta
    during the Olympics in 1996.

He was never charged with the crime
  or even officially called a suspect.
But for weeks, the F.B.I. followed him everywhere he went.
The news media were constantly on his trail.
Anytime he stepped out of his door,
  he was confronted by TV cameras and microphones.
In the midst of all this adversity,
    there was one place he found complete acceptance,
    and that was his mother's apartment.
There he found a safe haven, refuge, and compassion
    where he was always given the benefit of the doubt.

Today, let us thank God for our own family.
May we find in this community a safe haven for them,
    where the peace of Christ rules our hearts,
    and where the Word of Christ dwells in us richly.
With gratitude in our hearts and songs on our lips,
    may we come to this Eucharist as God's family,
    his chosen ones, holy and beloved.

A Glimpse of Fr. Hayes

We were asked to be godparents by proxy to my nephew's new baby. His pastor in southern Iowa asked that he have our pastor send him a letter stating that we were Catholics in good standing. This is what Fr. Mike wrote on Holy Angels letterhead for us to send. It was hand-written, of course.

To whom it may concern:

I have to congratulate the parents of Jerry Barnett for asking Brian and Regina Garvey to be sponsors. The parents have great judgement, and a touch of class. If I was a father to be, I would ask them, too.

Ego sum,
Michael T. Hayes, Pastor
                    —Regina Garvey, Parishioner of Holy Angels, Moose Lake, MN

Num 6:22–27; Gal 4:4–7; Lk 2:16–21

The Bird of Dawning Singeth

In the first act of Hamlet,
    after the ghost vanishes at the crowing of the sunrise rooster,
    the soldier Marcellus muses about the power of
    "the bird of dawning"
        to drive such fearful things away.
And he speaks of Christmas…
    Some say that ever 'gainst that season comes
    Wherein our Savior's birth is celebrated,
    The bird of dawning singeth all night long:
    And then, they say, no spirit can walk abroad;
    The nights are wholesome; then no planets strike,
    No fairy takes, nor witch hath power to charm,
    So hallow'd and so gracious is the time.

                —William Shakespeare, Hamlet, Act 1, Scene 2

The world gets older and older
    but this birth is always new.
And I am welcoming God
    and God is welcoming me.
The world is hallowed,
    a mystery and a wonder,
    but I understand it in my heart
        beyond sense.
Like the way one gets a joke, or doesn't get it.
You can't explain it;
    you either laugh or you don't.
At the darkest time of the year
    the light breaks through.
We've known it for thousands of years, even before Christ,
    and we've called it by thousands of names down the millennia.

We call it God, incarnation, Christ-Mass, Christmas.
We honor Mary with the title
    "Mother of God"
    because she is the mother of Jesus.
Without her,
    Jesus could not have been born into our world.
There would be no Emmanuel, no Christ-Mass; no Christmas.

Listen to this story about the importance of Mary.
The Catholic priest and the Protestant minister of the town
    decided that it would be nice
    to put a Christmas crib in the town square.
So they drew up a list of businesspeople
    from whom they would solicit donations
    to pay for the project.
One of the businesspeople on the priest's list
    was the editor of the town's weekly newspaper.
When the priest met with the editor,
    he said, "Our children will be inspired at seeing us
    give Jesus, Mary, and Joseph
    the place of honor in our town square."
The editor said, "I agree,
    but let's leave Mary out of the crib scene,
    because giving her such a prominent place in the town square
    might give children the impression
    that we're favoring your Catholic religion."
The priest responded,
    "I'll be glad to leave Mary out of the scene—
    if you will tell our children
    how Jesus could have been born without her."

Mary's oldest title is *Theotokos,* meaning "God-bearer."
Mary cannot be left out
    because an essential human aspect at the heart of our faith
    is that God chose a woman, Mary
        to realize his incarnation.

As we begin this New Year, let us together with the whole Church,
    renew our devotion to Mary, Mother of God.
Some of us may find deep spiritual satisfaction
    in renewing the custom of praying the Angelus,
        a magnificent summation of our faith.
Traditionally this prayer was said morning, noon, and night
    to recall the mystery of the Incarnation.
During this New Year, prayerfully renewing that simple devotion
    could transform our lives by putting us in touch
        with the paschal mystery of our own
        life, death, and resurrection.

So as we begin the New Year,
    let us be one with Mary, the Mother of God,
    as we recall together the beautiful mystery of God's love for us
    illuminated in the Angelus.
We will use this prayer as the Creed for today's Mass.

Priest	The angel of the Lord declared to Mary
All	And she conceived of the Holy Spirit.
	Recite the Hail Mary.
Priest	Behold the handmaid of the Lord
All	Let it be done to me according to your Word.
	Recite the Hail Mary.
Priest	The Word was made flesh
All	And dwelt among us.
	Recite the Hail Mary.
Priest	Let us pray: *Pour forth, we beseech you, your grace into our hearts, that we to whom the Incarnation was made known by the message of an angel, may by his passion and death be brought to the glory of the resurrection. Through Christ our Lord.*
All	Amen.

Isa 60:106; Eph 3:2–3a, 5–6; Mt 2:1–12

Darkness

"A cold coming we had of it.
Just the worst time of year for a journey—
   and such a long journey."
Rosemary Haughton is a well-known author.
In an article on the Epiphany,
   she begins by pointing out that for wise men,
   the Magi made a lot of mistakes!
They began their search by looking in all the wrong places.
They assumed that
   the fate of nations is decided by people of power.
And so they turned to King Herod for help.
The Magi had seen the star.
They were wise enough to know that it offered hope.
But they were not wise enough to see the danger
   and the evil of those whose only concern
   was for their own power and importance.

The Wise Men failed to be wary of darkness.
But despite the perils and mistakes of their journey,
   the Wise Men achieved their hope
   and found the child in a most unexpected place.
In the presence of the Child, they knew the meaning of the star.
In the presence of the Child, they also found wisdom
     to be wary of darkness.
So they returned home another way.
   Two roads diverged in a wood, and I—
   I took the one less traveled by,
   And that has made all the difference. (Robert Frost)
Yet even their silence and discretion was not protection enough.
Herod and his men sought the life of the Child.

Darkness was threatened by the star,
      and darkness attempted to extinguish the light.
The story of the Wise Men is the mystery of the Epiphany,
      the mystery of hope that we celebrate today.
The light of God continues to shine in the world,
      enabling us to continue our journey, too,
      despite the darkness that attempts to engulf and extinguish it.
"I have loved the stars too fondly
      to be fearful of the night." (Sarah William)

The Epiphany teaches us about darkness.
We learn that those who had studied the Scriptures,
      who knew about Bethlehem and the coming of the Messiah,
      were the ones who chose the darkness and refused the star, the light.
Darkness does not come only from fate or bad luck.
Darkness can be of our own making.
Sometimes the worst darkness
      comes into our life from human ill will and evil.
The Epiphany also teaches us that even human injustice
      does not quench the light of God.

The Epiphany teaches us wisdom.
Wisdom teaches us not to lose hope in the dark.
The star both appears and disappears from the Magi's sight,
      but they continued on their journey.
They did not lose hope.
Sometimes we see our way on life's journey clearly
      and then there are times we fail to pierce the dark and feel lost.
When that happens, we must not lose hope,
      but have the courage to continue our search for life's answers
            in our difficult times, too.
"This bird of dawning singeth all night long." (Hamlet, Act 1)

The Epiphany also teaches us about the wrong places to look for help!
It's not the places of power that count,
      but the places of love.

You can find light and love
    even in places of poverty and weakness.
Light comes from love, compassion, generosity, and courage.
Light comes from giving.

The Epiphany reveals that the Christ, the Jewish Messiah,
    had come not only for the Jews but for the whole world.
This story of the Magi was an early signal
    that the Church of Christ would be universal.
This is the feast of outsiders,
    of peoples of all races and colors.
It is a feast to help us realize that God intended variety.
The variety of races and colors on our earth
    is for enrichment and enjoyment
    and not a reason for hatred and division.
Racism is the greatest kind of perversion,
    an insult to the Creator who made us.
"Let your light shine," Jesus said.
Maybe this is the feast that asks you to guide others, possibly an outsider,
    to a meeting place with Christ.

The Epiphany teaches us to bring gifts.
The Magi came to seek and to worship.
They came to pay homage.
They came with open hearts,
    to recognize one greater than themselves.
So as we celebrate this Eucharist together,
    let's have the wisdom to bring gifts.
We may not have gold, frankincense, and myrrh,
    but we give bread and wine,
        products of our work and love.
We come with open hearts
    to recognize one greater than ourselves.
In the hands of Christ,
    our work and our love become his
    and in return, he becomes a gift back to us.
He becomes our light, our wisdom, and our hope.

Isa 55:1–11; Acts 10:34–38; Mt 3:13–17

I Am Sorry, My Brother, But I Have Nothing

The life of Jesus was a thing of beauty.
He is the supreme example of what a human life ought to be.
But that is the place where many draw the line.
They admire him,
    but entertain no thoughts of living as he lived.
To do that seems as impossible
    as painting another "Mona Lisa."
In a sense, that is true: Jesus is unique,
    but we cannot leave the matter there.
Jesus is not simply a lovely picture to be admired.

In an imperfect world, but practical sense,
    we can live as Jesus lived.
Obviously, Jesus did some things that we can never do.
"He went about doing good
    and healing all who were oppressed by the devil." (Acts 10:36)
Apparently, the miraculous deeds of Jesus
    are beyond our reach.
    "He went about doing good." (Acts 10:36)
That is more in our league—
    no miracles, or spectacular results,
    just the simple doing of useful things.

Jesus did things for the benefit of others.
    and everyone can live like that.
We have plenty of opportunities.
They cross our path everyday
    at home, at work, at school, on the street.

Our reading tells us that Jesus did good as he "went about."
I think that this means in the pursuit of his everyday life
    and that much of his ministry was almost accidental.
He did not go out looking for it.
But he was so aware of people
    that when an opportunity crossed his path, he saw it.
That is how he ended up helping the woman of Samaria.
You recall the occasion:
    the two of them met at a well.
It was not by appointment, or by design:
    they just met.
Jesus was there, resting from his journey,
    and the woman came to draw water.
Jesus engaged her in conversation,
    and ended up changing her life.
She was badly in need of a friend
    and Jesus became that friend.

We can live as Jesus lived by simply becoming more aware of people.
    Don't just walk past them.
    Look at them.
    See them.
    Listen to them.
Recognize their need,
    and take advantage of the opportunity to do them good.
Not only do we have plenty of opportunities,
    we also have adequate resources.
One of the main reasons many people fail to help
    is that they feel inadequate.
What can I do?
None of us is so poor that we cannot help somebody.

Do you remember this story about Leo Tolstoy?
On the streets of Moscow,
    he met a beggar, asking for money.
Tolstoy reached into his purse, but it was empty.

Ashamed that he had raised the hopes of a poor man,
    he put his hand on the man's shoulder.
Then, looking into his face, he said,
    "I'm sorry, my brother, but I have nothing."
The beggar replied,
"You have helped me more than you know.
You touched me,
    and you called me brother."
Even when our pockets are empty, we can give friendship.
All it takes is a little time and effort.
We have plenty of opportunities.
We have adequate resources
    and we also have the responsibility.

I am a priest.
It is my job to help.
But I can't do your helping for you.
None of us has a right to take care of only ourselves.
The priesthood is suffering from a lack of candidates
    and you may be called to share the ministry
        far more than in the past.
Part of the answer may be for people to exercise their own priesthood,
conferred on them by baptism
    and reaffirmed in confirmation.
Jesus said,
    "As the Father has sent me, so do I send you."

A few years ago, a remarkable film was released around the U.S.
Imagine a movie that doesn't apologize
    for the religious journey of its central character.
Entertaining Angels is such a movie,
    and it is the story of Dorothy Day.
She was the founder of the Catholic Worker Movement
    and she is often referred to as the "American Mother Teresa"
        for her work with the poor.

In the movie, Miss Day is shown as a young woman
   who demonstrated against social injustice
   and whose freewheeling lifestyle
      resulted in her having an abortion
      and later becoming a single parent.
Gradually she is drawn to the social mission of the Church
   and baptized along with her child.

In one of the film's most moving scenes,
   Miss Day is alone in a church in front of a statue of Jesus.
She asks the Lord about the gospel's call
   to see Christ in those most rejected by society.
"Let me tell you something.
   They smell. They have lice, and tuberculosis.
   Am I to find you in them?" she asks.
The answer she received is:
   "Yes."
Miss Day went on to serve the poor and to fight injustice
   until she died in 1980 at the age of eighty-three.
More than a hundred Catholic Worker soup kitchens and shelters
   continue her work.

Our baptism calls us to be the servants of all.
Living like Jesus is our highest calling
   and our deepest worship.
Someone is calling you!

Lent & Easter

Joel 2:12–18; 2 Cor 5:20—6:2; Mt 6:1–6, 16–18

The Recycling Bin of Lent

"You've got dirt on your forehead."
You may hear those words from a thoughtful friend
    as they display their concern.
It is something like being told you have jam or ketchup on your face. Your
friend saying, "You've got dirt on your forehead,"
    might also be displaying his or her religious absent-mindedness.
There is no penitential rite at this Mass.
Instead of merely calling to mind our sins,
    we receive a very public reminder of our sinfulness.

"Will you turn away from sin and be faithful to the gospel?"
The answer is, "I will."

In the early Church only public sinners wore ashes.
But in 1091, Pope Urban II ordered up the first Ash Wednesday
    and we've been rubbing dirt on our foreheads ever since.

Dirt is something we are constantly washing off
    our children and ourselves.
Only in the church do we deliberately put ashes—dirt—
    on the most public part of our bodies: our foreheads.
Ashes are what's left in a now-cold fireplace.
Ashes heat the barbecue.
Ashes are all that remains of a house after a tragic fire.
Ashes enrich the compost heap.
Ashes of the departed fill commemorative urns.
Ashes represent destruction, refuse, and waste.
But ashes are also the hint of new life.

Long before recycling became popular,
  the Church got into the act on Ash Wednesday.
Do you ever wonder what happens to the palm branches
  left over from last year's Holy Week?
They have been burned to dirty your forehead this Ash Wednesday.

The symbol of Christ's glory
  has become the symbol of our sin.

On Ash Wednesday, you're not just another dirty face.
No, you've tossed yourself into the recycling bin of Lent,
  ready for renewal this Easter.

Gen 9:8–15; 1 Pet 3:18–22; Mk 1:12–15

Calmly Plotting the Resurrection

American writer E.B. White is best known
   as the author of the children's classic, *Charlotte's Web,*
   but he is also famous for other writings.
In a piece that was written late in his life,
   he mused about his wife's gardening:
"As the years went by and age overtook her,
   there was something comical yet touching
      in her bedraggled appearance on this awesome occasion…
   the small hunched-over figure,
   her studied absorption in the implausible notion
      that there would be yet another spring,
   oblivious to the ending of her own days,
      which she knew perfectly well as near at hand,
   sitting there with her detailed chart
   under those dark skies in the dying October,
      calmly plotting the resurrection."

"Calmly plotting the resurrection";
   that is the perfect description
   of what we will be doing in this lenten season.
The seeds we plant now will grow and blossom come Easter Day.
But it is difficult to believe that promise.
Lent is meant to touch and change us, yet we find it hard to move on.
But move on we must.

The promise of resurrection will overcome our anxiety.
All we have to do is move on,
>and Lent is the way of taking the first step
>out of the dingy rooms in which we have been living.
We can take the risk of moving because of the promise.
We may now only dimly perceive Easter
>and hear its faint music.
But we do see a little
>and we do hear a bit—
>just enough to give us courage.

In Lent forgiveness is larger than sin;
>even our dullness will not be held against us.
God will truly do a new thing in our lives.
Lent calls us to redecorate
>the spiritual space in which we live.
Too long we have gone without enough love and mercy.
Those things waste away if we do not use them.

Lent is our time of exercise.
It is a time in which we stop blaming other people and other things,
>and own up to our past, confident of forgiveness.
We leave behind the furniture of cynicism,
>the dirty rugs,
>the dreary colors,
>and windows painted shut.
We move into a new room
>where the windows are open wide to change
>and the colors shift with the light of Christ that flows in.

If we really mean it,
>we are putting ourselves in a place where we will be changed
>>as we go about "plotting the resurrection."

In Lent, hope turns real and we are challenged
>"to mean what we are meant to be,
>to go where we are meant to go." (Maya Angelou)

Gen 22:1–4a; Rom 8:31b–34; Mk 9:2–10

It's So Beautiful There

"Rabbi, it is good to be here." (Mark 9:4)

Psychiatrist and writer Gerald May
    vividly recalls his first near-death encounter,
    during his medical school days.
On this particular evening a man who had been stabbed
    was brought to the emergency room.
He had lost a great deal of blood
    and died on the table in the emergency room.
Dr. May started administering CPR
    and the man responded favorably.
But as soon as he regained consciousness,
    he slugged Dr. May, knocking him down.
His words to Dr. May somewhat explained his actions.
"You take me away from that?
    You take me away from that?
    How dare you take me away from that!"
The event reminded Dr. May of what his own father said
    just before he died:
        "It's so beautiful there."

"Near death" experiences have become common in our day.
There are people who stand on the verge of dying completely,
    but they recover and report fascinating sights.
Many are reluctant to come back to this life
    and wish the journey towards the next had continued.
Recent studies have renamed the experiences
    "near life" experiences.

Death is not an end,
   but rather a change from one form of life
   to what appears to be a higher form.
This "new" insight echoes the age-old tradition
   Paul captured in his letter to the Romans:
"For I am convinced that neither death nor life nor anything else
   will be able to separate us
   from the love of God in Christ Jesus our Lord." (Rom 8:39)
This insight is repeated in the funeral liturgy,
   "Life is changed, not taken away."

The transfiguration reported in today's gospel
   could be placed in the category of "near life" experiences.
Jesus and three intimate friends
   see another dimension of life.
We see Peter communicating to Jesus
   sentiments similar to people who experience "near death."

Peter doesn't slug Jesus.
He didn't he say, "How dare you take me away from that."
But he obviously was saying,
   "It's so beautiful here and I want to stay."
"Let us make three dwellings,
   one for you, one for Moses, and one for Elijah." (Mark 9:5)

But Peter soon discovered that he could stay there.
He had to come down from the mountain
   and face the reality of everyday living, like the rest of us.
"Suddenly, when they looked around
   they saw no one with them any more, but only Jesus." (Mark 9:8)

At the beginning of a relationship
   most people experience what is called romantic love.
There is a similarity between this experience
   and the gospel experience.
Many do not realize that romantic love has a beginning and an end.
Romantics want to stay there forever.

But when it ends, mature love begins,
    and it is time to come down from the mountain
    and face the struggle of everyday living.
One of the reasons soap operas are so popular
    is because they offer the viewer an escape
    from the difficult challenge
    of dealing with their own relationships in the reality of daily life.
The weekend can be a real high,
    but then comes Monday morning
    and we have to come down from the mountain.
We have to think about earning a living and paying the bills.

Around this time of the year the weather can give us a high,
    a feeling of spring with longer days and shorter nights.
But we can also get a blast of cold reality
    that reminds us we are still experiencing winter.

Some people turn to drugs
    looking for the high experienced by Peter in today's gospel,
        but they don't find it.
They crash into reality and pay a high price for the experiment.
But there is a very important point about today's gospel
    that could be easily missed.
Peter's experience of the transfiguration
    was indeed something very special.
But when "they come down from the mountain,"
    they were not leaving the presence of God.
God was still with them.

Sometimes when we move
    from romantic love to a more mature love,
    from a feeling of closeness to God
        to a feeling of being abandoned by God,
    from a sunny day to a rainy day,
    we have a tendency to forget that God is with us all the time.

It may seem as if God is gone.
It may seem as if God is not responding,
    and this really hurts.
When we are tempted,
    we don't feel like we are on top of the mountain
        in communion with God.
But God is with us before, during, and after the temptation.
We need to remember this.

God endlessly protects our freedom to say "yes" or "no,"
    and when we say "yes" we grow in love.
We become who we really are
    and who we are meant to be.
When we are tested, it is good to remember
    that God is with us as we struggle.

Exod 20:1–17 or 20:1–3, 7–8, 12–17; 1 Cor 1:22–25; Jn 2:13–25

The Whip of Cords

"Zeal for your house will consume me." (John 2:17)

Jesus slashed downward
    with the whip he had made from thick cords.
The whip cracked hard across a table,
    overturning it, and spilling everything out onto the floor.
Jesus was breathing hard as he shouted,
"Stop making my Father's house a marketplace!" (John 2:16)
He was clutching the whip so tightly
    that he had to remind himself to relax his grip.
It is an image in stark contrast
    to the meek and mild picture of Jesus
        put into our religious memory from early childhood.

We see Jesus angry.
We see his north side.
The once business-like order of the temple
    was now a scene of chaos.
Escaping doves fluttered overhead.
Untethered oxen were wandering
    through the jumble of tables and boxes
    as Jesus surveyed the aftermath of his work.
Some are troubled by this scene. Why would Jesus get angry?
There is fear that this shows him as too "human."

The money changers, the ancient equivalent of the ATM,
    were still scrambling to find all the coins
    that were spilled when Jesus overturned their table.
Other vendors were rolling up their wares and retreating.

A crowd of onlookers had quickly gathered.
One man from the crowd, hoping to see a fight, shouted at Jesus,
    "Who do you think you are with your whip and your big mouth?"
Another voice added: "He must be crazy."
"Get the rabbi," another shouted.
Jesus knew their hearts.
They had little time for God.
They had little concern for their temple
    which had been reduced to a public market.
They had even less interest in the message of Jesus.
There was a pall of hopelessness about the scene,
    but they would all be back in the morning.
Business as usual.

Someone asked,
    "What sign can you show us authorizing you to do these things?"
Even then, the people were interested in credentials.
    "Who are you?
    Show us your badge, your card.
    To whom do you answer?
    Prove yourself to us!"
Jesus turned to him and answered,
    "Destroy this temple," he began, placing his hands on his own chest
    to indicate he was talking about the temple of his body,
    "and in three days I will raise it up." (John 3:19)
A ripple of laughter went through the crowd.
One of them, thinking Jesus was talking
    about the temple building, said,
"This temple has been under construction for forty-six years
    and will you raise it up in three days?" (John 3:20)
Jesus smiled back and nodded.
The disciples who were with Jesus would one day recall
    the great resurrection prophecy that day by Jesus.

Lent charges into our lives once a year, overturning our tables.
Lent challenges us to think about
    our interests, our positions, and our transgressions.

Lent asks us to examine the way we live,
    and the integrity of our relationship with God.
During Lent, we may uncover obstacles
    which keep us from living our faith to the fullest.

Jesus asks us,
    "What is this doing in your life?
    Get it out; it's blocking your path to me."
Then Jesus will hand us his whip of cords
    so we can use it to drive the obstacles away,
    those things in the temple of our hearts
        that need "driving out" this Lent.

2 Chr 36:14–16, 19–23; Eph 2:4–10; Jn 3:14–21

DOORS

"And I, when I am lifted up from the earth,
will draw all people to myself." (John 12:33)

There is a silent sermon spoken by the silhouette
    of each Celtic cross with a cross and crown intertwined
    seen so often in the Irish graveyards.
As a latter-day prophet, Kahlil Gibran, said,
"The deeper sorrow carves into your being,
    the more joy you can obtain."

Laetare or "rejoicing Sunday"
    is the midpoint of our lenten observance.
It's almost as if we need a little joy in the midst
    of this somber and penitential season of preparation for Easter.
The joy of Easter breaks into our lenten experience.
(The other time will be St. Patrick's Day!)
But it is still Lent, of course, and the liturgy reflects that.
The Glory to God and the Alleluia are still banished,
    but some flowers appear this Sunday,
    for a taste of Spring and a foretaste of Easter.
Lest the hint of Easter becomes much more than a hint,
    remember that, although the flowers are beautiful,
    they are only a hint of what will appear at Easter.
And be cautioned:
    when Easter comes too quickly
    it dismisses the pain without healing it.

Lent is about doors that open and shut.

One day during rush hour,
    a New York subway train pulled into the station.
The train came to a stop, but the doors would not open.
Time passed and the conductor finally made an announcement:
    "This train is out of service due to a mechanical problem.
    The doors will not open. Please leave the train immediately."
Rusty bolts, mechanical failure:
    sometimes the doors just will not open.

In the scene from which today's gospel is taken,
    that is Nicodemus' problem
    and the answer is in today's gospel text.
"For God so loved the world that he gave his only Son,
    so that everyone who believes in him may not perish,
    but may have eternal life." (John 3:16)
That one verse,
    so often quoted and misquoted, used and abused,
    is the heart that beats at the center of our faith.
It's the wedge that works away in the crevices of our hearts
    to open the door.
Even a stuck door offers a slight opening
    to the master of doors.

But beware of psychological crutches.
There is an idolatry abroad that says
    you open your own doors.
These days we hear a lot about new spiritualities
    in and outside of the Church:
    charisma, karma, New Age beliefs, Eastern mysticism,
    depth psychology and dreams, tarot cards and crystals,
    certain foods and practices, even visions and miracles.
Yet there are many ways to God,
    and even while retaining respect,
    there are some things we easily notice.
It is easy to notice that some approaches come close
    to magic and superstition.

It is easy to notice approaches
    that are in no way concerned with justice.
They show no concern for other people.
It is easy to notice approaches that focus us on self.
The world would have us seek our own perfection,
    our own removal from the pain of life.

It's easy to notice, too, that such approaches
    describe spirituality as a perfection we attain
        by unleashing our own potential.
But we should look for the action of God
    in our time and in our lives,
    at our own doors.

Lent invites us to put our ears up against the door
    and take shallow breaths
    so that we can catch God in the act.
Otherwise, we will miss the revelation.
God may be active but we will not see it:
    God loved and sent.
The core of reality is not what we do, but what God does.

Doors can open from the inside or from the outside.
When the doorknob on the inside of a door falls off,
    we can lock ourselves in: this is how God works.
Our doors may be stuck from our side,
    but God can still open them.
For all we know, the door may be open now.
Have you checked your door lately?

Maybe you think you are locked in
    without realizing how free God has made you!
In this Eucharist, the God who is comes to open our doors.
Welcome this God.
Cead mile Failte!
    ("A hundred thousand welcomes" in Gaelic.)

Jer 31:31–34; Heb 5:7–9; Jn 12:20–33

The World's Saddest Story

Because next Sunday's passion reading leaves little time for a homily,
    and the whole story of Holy Week
      is just too much to assimilate during the week itself,
      I would like to focus today on the passion of Jesus,
      to set in motion some serious thoughts for the coming season.
The meaning and depth of the sufferings of Jesus
      were summed up profoundly, but simply,
      by a farmer many years ago in a remote Irish village.
He looked at the crucifix hanging on the wall behind the altar
      on Good Friday and exclaimed,
      "To think that the likes of him would do the likes of that
        for the likes of me."

The cross is a gathering place for sorrow.
Eventually, life brings us all here.
Yet a strange hope is possible in this assembly.
It is not the hope of an easy Easter, or a ready response:
      when Easter comes too quickly,
        it dismisses the pain of the cross
          and thus we are left without healing.
We try to avoid the struggle.
But the cross seems to be in everybody's lexicon of lament and grief.
It's the key that fits but does not unlock the door,
      the core piece of the puzzle we put in place
      before the tomb is unsealed.
The strange hope of the cross is not Easter.
It is hope that comes from merely having a place to gather
      when the pain is unspeakable
      and the sorrow beyond bearing.

Sometimes darkness needs darkness for a while.
When the light is premature, it does not illuminate or heal.
It startles us and we turn away in pain.

In his poem "The Divine Comedy,"
    Dante at long last beholds God only after having borne
    the darkness of the inferno and the shadows of Purgatory.
God appears as light,
    a light brilliant, and yet somehow bearable for mortal eyes.
This light, Dante tells us,
    bright beyond all definition, did not blind.
Indeed, he says,
    to turn from such a light would be blindness.
And so he stares, transfixed,
    unable to turn away,
    straining ever more ardently to absorb the light.
Such light and such commitment to it
    would not help before the prior darkness is experienced.

The cross is the gathering place for the world's sorrows.
It is Christianity's most believable symbol.
The loss of God on the cross calls us to a God
    far above the God of the lilies of the field.
Such a God seems inadequate
    to the gas chambers and ovens of the Jewish Holocaust,
    to the starvation and death of the Irish Holocaust,
    the famine of 1847,
    to the horrid light and heat of Hiroshima,
    to a world where eighty percent of the human family
    is compelled to survive with only twenty percent of its resources.

Sometimes the world's sorrows seem bigger
    than the God of the lilies and sparrows.
If this be the only God there is,
    then we may abandon such an easy God
    for one more adequate to our pain.

The Christ who died in anguish
> gathers all the tormented children of the world.

Sr. Mary Rose McGready of Covenant House,
> a shelter for youth in New York City, tells this story.

"Nobody wants these kids," she says of the youth at Covenant House.
"Their families don't want them.
The system doesn't want them.
The government doesn't want them.
Except for the fact that we've 700,000 Americans who support us,
> we wouldn't be able to do any of this."

"Sister, how much do you get paid to take care of me?" the boy asked.
He was sixteen years old, a little desperate and very tired.
"I mean how much does the state give you? Do they give you a lot?"
"Now, why did you ask that question?"
"Well, that's what my mother said when she threw me out.
She said she got money from the state
> for the foster children she took in
> and if I was gone she could take in one more foster child."

The Christ who died in anguish gathers all the unused graces,
> and shattered dreams, all the world's wasted efforts.

There is a place for us when our soul weeps.
We find comfort in the cross,
> in the silence,
> in the darkness,
> in our aversion to the light,
> in our need to have no immediate answers.
Let us gather for a moment in the silence,
> not yet healed.
Do not try to heal us yet.
Let us only be together.

We can wait as long as we are not alone,
> at the place where God lost everything.

At the cross we seem to be able to endure
   not because Easter is believable,
   but because loss connects us with everyone.
We can wait.
We choose to wait.
We prefer to wait,
   as long as we are not alone—
   and as long as we know that it is not only us, but God who dies.
"Unless a grain of wheat falls into the earth and dies
   it remains just a single grain;
   but if it dies, it bears much fruit." (John 12:24)

In rural Ireland there is still a custom
   of sowing potatoes on Good Friday,
      a custom that hardly needs to be explained.
We are invited to participate in the passion and death of Christ,
   and to bear witness to that suffering in our own lives.

Isa 50:4–7; Phil 2:6–11; Mk 14:1, 15–47

This Week of Love

Zechariah had prophesied that the Messiah
   would ride into Jerusalem on a donkey.
Our modern Western notion of a donkey is not a flattering one.
We think of a donkey as a stupid animal.
G.K. Chesterton popularized this notion in a poem.
In it he has the donkey reflect on its ugliness and say to itself:

> When fishes flew and forests walked
> And figs grew upon thorn,
> Some moment when the moon was blood
> Then surely I was born.
>
> With monstrous head and sickening cry
> And ears like errant wings,
> The devils walking parody
> On all four-footed things.
>
> Fools! For I also had my hour,
> One far fierce hour and sweet:
> There was a shout about my ears
> And palms before my feet.

And so the donkey says in effect:
   "You modern people may ridicule and mock me,
   But of all the animals on earth,
   I was the chosen
   To carry on my back the savior of the world."

People in biblical times honored the donkey.
The donkey was an animal of peace
    as opposed to the horse, which was an animal of war,
      carrying soldiers into battle.
Jesus' act of riding into Jerusalem on an animal of peace
    says that an important part of the Messiah's mission
    would not be to rally people to their cause
    and drive the Romans out of Palestine into the sea.
Jesus wasn't going to be a warrior-king,
    to sit on a throne and be served by conquered Romans.
Instead, he came to kneel on the floor
    and wash the feet of his subjects.
Jesus didn't to do battle against other people.
He wasn't riding on a horse.
He has come to rally them behind him
    and do battle against poverty, hunger, hatred,
      and all forms of injustice.

Jesus hasn't come to condemn people.
He has come to forgive them.
Jesus hasn't come to destroy people's dreams.
He has come to fulfill them
    in the most wonderful way imaginable.
It is this Jesus whom we greet today.

The Passion According to Mark

We can't help but focus on the sufferings and death of Christ.
But this is not the primary focus of the liturgy.
As Christians we do not celebrate death.
We only celebrate life and love.

As Christian people we do not celebrate the dying of Jesus.
We recall it,
    we remember it,
    we groan because of it,
    we repent because of our part in it:
"Father, forgive us, for we were there when they crucified our Lord."

But we do not celebrate it.
I repeat: we only celebrate life and love.
Our liturgical celebration today is a celebration of the Risen Christ,
    the Risen Jesus.
He died, but rose to new life as we rise to new life.
This is our faith.

In this liturgy we will hear the change of focus from death to life,
    when the celebrant says,
"In memory of his death and resurrection,
    we offer you, Father, this life-giving bread, this saving cup."
It is this Jesus who wants to enter our hearts in a special way
    during this week of love.
Let us go forth in peace, praising Jesus, our messiah,
    as did the crowds who welcomed him to Jerusalem.

A Glimpse of Fr. Hayes

As a twenty-fifth anniversary gift to ourselves, my husband and I went to Ireland. While traveling in the west of that lovely land (between Lahinch and Bunratty Castle) we befriended a couple who shared our last name. They owned a pub aptly name Garvey's. Their sign drew us to its doors and hence, its owners. This was in the little town of Inagh.

A few years later the Irish Garveys came to visit us at our home in Moose Lake. It happened to be Wednesday of Holy Week when they arrived. Fr. Mike had been awaiting their arrival almost as anxiously as we had and joined us for dinner Thursday evening after Mass. Mike was anxious to give these travelers from his homeland a special treat and offered to bring Irish rashers (bacon) for breakfast the next morning. He had been saving this in his freezer for some time waiting for just the right occasion. We had a wonderful breakfast on Good Friday, and I believe he came up with a few words about dispensation for all of us, as we were entertaining travelers, you know.

—Regina Garvey, Parishioner of Holy Angels Parish, Moose Lake, MN

Exod 12:1–8, 11–14; 1 Cor 11:23–26; Jn 13:1–15

This Is No Snack Bar

"Bless us, O Lord, and these your gifts
    which we are about to receive…."

When you go to McDonalds, Pizza Hut, or KFC,
    you go there to eat.
You may go to a restaurant for a variety of reasons,
    but the main reason for walking through the door is to eat.
You don't go there to become friendly with the management
    and agree that you will never eat anyplace else.
You make no promise that you will do everything they tell you
    for the rest of your life.
You will pay for your meal
    and not throw French fries at the customers.
But that is about it.

And it surely goes without saying that you make no commitment to
    the cow, the chicken, and the anchovy you consume.
You are not eating them to become like them in looks or habits.
Some people say, "You are what you eat."
I doubt any of us literally are.
I might eat baloney and become full of it,
    but I doubt if I take on the looks and lifestyle
    of all those poor creatures whose meat is in that baloney.

It is a very different story when you receive Communion,
    when you eat his body, drink his blood at this Mass.
You are putting yourself in the position of making
    an agreement,
    a covenant,
    a commitment.

When you eat and drink of Jesus,
    you are promising that you will live the rest of your life
    doing what Jesus tells you to do.
You are saying to the management of heaven
    that you want to become like Jesus.
We declare that we wish to become like Jesus.

Jesus sets an example and directs his disciples to do as he has done.
He washes the feet of his disciples, and tells them,
    "Do as I have done."
We are to give ourselves over to a life of washing one another's feet.
In countless ways we are to care,
    to love, to serve, and to bear one another's burdens.
And so we declare in our "Amens"
    to the body of Christ,
    to the blood of Christ,
        that we wish to become like Jesus.

Our Communion is no snack bar,
    no fast food joint,
    not even an elegant country club dining room.
This is where you come to partake of the body and blood of Christ
    and promise that whatever he tells you, you will listen.
You will try your utmost to abide by it—
    at least you will try very hard.
Amen: I will strive to become what I eat and drink.
This is not a snack,
    but the main meal for our lives,
    and we are placing ourselves in the position
        of becoming what we eat.
We allow God to form in us the likeness of his Son.

And so this eating place where you have come
    is not just another among many.
It is not a place that brags
    about the billions who have been served—
        even if it is true.

But at our table is served
    the best of all food,
    the catch of the day,
    and we will never have to change the special of the day.

May you become very aware of what it is
    you eat and drink.
When you dine here,
    we have the food that is the source of life.

Bless us, O Lord and these your gifts
which we are about to receive….

Bless us, and help us become what we eat and drink.

Isa 52:13, 53:12; 1 Cor 11:23–26; Jn 13:1–15

The Paschal Mystery

The celebration of Christ's life, death, and resurrection
   is too big to celebrate in one day, three days,
      or even fifty days.
We need a lifetime to remember and rejoice.

  April is the cruelest month, breeding
  Lilacs out of the dead land, mixing
  Memory and desire, stirring
  Dull roots with Spring rain. (T.S. Eliot, "The Waste Land")

We gather this Friday evening as only a family in mourning can do.
Death has stunned us.
We are caught up in the tragedy.
Death. Everyone knew he was walking right into it.
Anguish, dying, death, pain, grief.
And on top of it so young a man, in his prime.
He had everything going for him.
Some say, "How tragic!" Others, "What a fool! Why die?"
The death of Jesus grips us.
It compels us to draw closer, while at the same time,
   we want to recoil, to run away.

But there is a gift about this death.
Memory haunts us,
   and calls us to the wake, to the awakening.
Here is the bittersweet of Jesus, our love.
The April fool, let down by friends, let down from the cross.
We have been able to stop everything to be here.
Here we are with Jesus in compassion, betrayal,
   pain, sorrow, and crucifixion.

In time, there will be thanksgiving,
    time together, time to remember, desire stirring.
After all we are only half awake.
There will be food to sustain us this day,
    gathered from last night's supper.
The heavy wooden cross turns into a mirror, a window.
It reflects war everywhere,
    hungry faces,
    starving eyes,
    no work,
    no home,
    no safety,
    no assurance of bread and cup today.

Here, there, everywhere
    people battered and addicted,
    power gone wrong
    and nature in upheaval:
    earthquake and fire, flood and storm,
    sin and fear, pain and evil.
We are strangers to no one in these regards.

There is dull, unrelenting pain,
    not unlike thorns and nails and shock.
Then the last blow.
The lance draws blood and water from the heart.
Blood and water at death—like blood and water at birth.
Which is it?
Birth unto death, like those lives lost in war,
    or death into birth?

His body was broken for you and me,
    for us, and for them.
And yes, baptismal water will flow at the Easter Vigil
    and there will be new blood in this old Church.
Fullness of life will be graced by the cup.

Yesterday, today, tomorrow—
    a mix of memory and desire,
    life unto death;
    death unto life.
Death is a comma, not a full stop.
Was he really as much of a fool as he appeared to be?

We are used to seeing the crucifixion as unfinished business,
    and as you just heard, the resurrection is also unfinished business.
A poet captures this unfinished business aspect very well.
She finds Jesus on the cross, unable to get down,
    and she, who presumably speaks for us all,
    volunteers to take the nail out.
But Jesus says,
    "Let them be,
    For I cannot be taken down
    Until every man, every woman,
        and every child
    Come together to take me down."
What can I do in the meantime, the poet wants to know.
Jesus gives the obvious answer,
    "Go about the world
    Tell everyone you meet,
    There is a man on the cross."

There is a continuity between crucifixion and resurrection.
That mystery we dare not collapse.
    "There is a man on the cross
    He is in the throes of labor, rising from the dead."
The End?
Not really.

Acts 10:34a, 37–43; Col 3:1–4; Jn 20:1–9

An Easter Invitation

The gospels do not explain the resurrection;
  the resurrection explains the gospels.

Women were the first to hear the message of Easter.
The inclusion of women in the ministry of Jesus was important
  not only to the women themselves,
    but because women, in the culture of Jesus' time, were inferior;
      they were possessions.
Women were simply not thought about as significant
  except as being useful to others.
The fact that it was women who first heard the message
  shows us the priorities of the Easter message.
This is not just about individual salvation;
  it is about the overturning of what St. Paul called
    "things as they are."
Important as Peter and other early church leaders soon became,
  the message was not given first of all to them.
On the contrary, they received it from the women.

It stands as witness to the priorities of Jesus,
  his own preferential option for the poor,
  his own insistence on inclusiveness
    without regard to income, gender, or professional status.
Life doesn't make sense unless we can make some sense out of death.
And death does not make sense without the resurrection.
Belief in the resurrection is not an appendage to the Christian faith:
  it *is* the Christian faith.
Now, here's an Easter story for you.
A man wandered into the local cemetery.
It was night and he was severely "under the influence."

He stumbled into an open grave and fell asleep.
When he awakened the next day, he was puzzled, to say the least.
He climbed to the top of the grave,
    looked around at all the tombstones, and exclaimed,
"My God, it's the resurrection. And I'm the first one up!"
This is the invitation of Easter.

Why not resurrect who you are, and give yourself new life?
It's the good news that we don't have to wait until death
    to share in the resurrection.
We can begin to do it right now
    in this life, at this moment, at this Mass.
Every time we love again after having our love rejected,
    we share in the power of the resurrection.
Every time we trust again after having our trust betrayed,
    we share in the power of the resurrection.
Each time we hope again after having our hopes smashed into pieces,
    we share in the power of the resurrection.

The message of Easter is that nothing can destroy us anymore:
    not pain, not sin, not rejection, not death.
It's the good news that every Good Friday
    now has an Easter Sunday.
The parting thoughts of the Eastern Orthodox Easter Vigil liturgy
    are the same each year.
They are in a reading from the fourth-century Easter sermon
    of St. John Chrysostom.
It is inclusive enough for all of us.
    Ye rich and poor, rejoice together.
    Ye sober and slothful, celebrate the day.
    Ye that have kept the fast and ye that have not,
    Rejoice today, for the table is richly laden.
    Let no one mourn that he had fallen again and again,
    For forgiveness has risen from the grave.
May this Alleluia echo in our hearts and deeds today
    and in the coming fifty days of Easter.

Acts 4:32-35; 1 Jn 5:1–6; Jn 20:19–31

Easter for Late-Bloomers

Let us proclaim the mystery of faith: "My Lord and my God."

No matter how long you stare at trees,
    you will never actually spot a sudden bloom.
It's when you look away
    that blossoms grow. (Measles, too!)
The disciple Thomas was a realist.
(I bet that when he was a kid,
    he stared at trees to spot a sudden bloom!)
Some people are just like that.
They need more than words and promises.

Thomas missed the Risen Lord the first time around.
The other disciples described the scene in vivid detail,
    but for Thomas, seeing was believing.
And what he saw wasn't very convincing.
After all, if Jesus had really risen and had appeared to the disciples,
    why were the doors still locked?
Why were they still hiding in the closet
    and not out on the streets proclaiming the good news?

Some pious preachers have even dubbed Thomas
    a poor community member
    because he wasn't with his brothers and sisters
    when the Risen Lord first appeared.
But perhaps what he lacked was not faith in God,
    but faith in the people around him.
Thomas may be like the saying,
    "Don't believe what you hear."

In a sense, we, like Thomas,
   have a hard time believing what surrounds us.
Thomas had no difficulty believing in Jesus.
   "My Lord and my God," he cries out.
But he did have a problem believing in his friends.
Thomas wanted more than words.

In today's gospel, Jesus gave the disciples hope.
He transformed his friends' fear and restored their belief
   by showing them his wounds.
What do we do with our wounds?
We hide them, fearful that others might see
   our weaknesses and vulnerability.
At times we even deny to ourselves that we are wounded.
We are afraid to share that we have been wounded by life.

In recent times we have seen how many innocent children
   were wounded by adults.
They had to carry deep scars which no one,
   not even their spouses, knew about.
Just as Thomas came to believe by seeing Jesus' wounds,
   we come to believe, and understand
   why some people are the way they are
   because of the wounds that life has inflicted upon them.

There will be times, like Thomas, when we have our doubts,
   but by being here we are testifying to our hope
   in the wounded Son of God,
   the Risen Savior Jesus Christ,
   our Lord and our God.

As you approach the altar to receive
   the wounded but resurrected body of Our Lord,
   show him your wounds.
Pray for the courage to show someone you trust your wounds,
   and for the humility to allow someone to show you theirs.

Peace be with you.
Today's gospel is telling us that our lives
    will include crucifixion and resurrection,
    death and life, fear and peace.
This is the peace of Christ
    that was extended to Thomas who doubted him,
    and that is available to each one of us today.

We may not know where society is going
    in its war against terrorism.
We may not know where the Church is going
    in its struggle to reform itself.
But we do know that the peace of Christ
    is available to us during this difficult time.
Like Thomas, our response is "My Lord and my God."

Acts 3:13–15, 17–19; 1 Jn 2:1–5a; Lk 24:35–48

A Messy, Ugly Place

Jesus told them to touch him.
He told them not to be afraid to touch him, since he was not a ghost.
He was the same Jesus they had kissed many times
    on both sides of the face,
    the way they had always greeted one another,
    and still greet one another in that part of the world.
It was the same Jesus they had rubbed elbows with
    at the Last Supper.
He was the same Jesus who often touched them,
    even their smelly feet, which he washed the night before
        his own feet were nailed to the cross.
Sometimes, especially when words fail,
    touch means everything.
"Touch me, and see, for a ghost does not have flesh and bones
    as you see that I have." (Luke 24:39)
Why in the world did the Risen Lord do that?!

Jesus died a messy, ugly death in a messy, ugly place.
There was no glamour on Golgotha, the "skull place."
There must have been a stench about the place—
    the stench of violent death,
    the stench of triumph,
    the stench of despair.
There were no sterilized needles here.
This only happens before a lethal injection in Texas
    where the guilty must be put to death humanely.

Peter blamed ignorance.
In the first reading, he says:

"I know that you acted in ignorance,
    as did also your rulers." (Acts 3:17)
Jesus eventually arose in triumph, victorious.
His post-resurrection body still carried the scars.
The gospel proclaims,
"Look at my hands and my feet;
    see that it is I myself." (Luke 24:39)
The Risen Lord was not a phantom, or a ghost.
This was the Jesus who rose in truth,
    the Jesus who had died on the cross.
Our Christian faith is founded on this physical fact,
    not on dreams and visions.
The cross was a necessary part of the plan,
    not an emergency measure when all else failed.

In a messy, ugly place, God's love shines through.
In fact it was the scars on the body of Jesus
    that helped the disciples to recognize him.
These Golgothas leave scars
    but the very scars can become badges of victory,
        signs of encouragement and hope, signs of resurrection.
The disciples left the upper room
    enthused, confident, full of hope!

May your trials keep you strong,
    your sorrows keep you human,
    your failures keep you humble.
May your hope keep you happy,
    your enthusiasm keep you looking forward.
May your faith banish depression,
    your wealth meet your needs,
and your friends give you comfort.
May you have, in the Risen Lord,
    determination to make each day better than yesterday.
And we pray that we might be ever more joyful, loving,
    and passionate witnesses of Jesus' resurrection story.

A Glimpse of Fr. Hayes

In the early 1980s, Fr. Hayes and St. Francis Parish decided to build a new rectory out in the country south of the town of Carlton, MN. The rectory was to be erected on ten acres just west of St. Francis Parish Center.

When Fr. Hayes told me that he had valued the old rectory at about $30,000, and that he was going to raffle it off with $100 chances, I thought he had embarked on a totally impossible task. I could not conceive that he would be able to sell all those chances on the dilapidated rectory in just a few months.

What happened is this: Mike sold chances for the old rectory for over a year. He broke the $100 dollar chances into smaller lots so that truck drivers and travelers from outside the region in bars and restaurants could buy chances. Mike banked the money he collected at the high-interest rates of the time, a time in which real estate values were declining in our area.

Finally, all the chances were sold, and a winner was selected at a gala party. Fr. Mike had banked over $32,000 in interest and raffle sales and the winner would sell his house in a declining real estate market for $26,000. I was astounded!

Fr. Hayes built a lovely new rectory while conducting a successful sale of the old rectory. I thought to myself, this man has extraordinary abilities in promotion and sales. I had never met a priest quite like him.

— Dr. John Connolly, Cloquet, MN

Acts 2:1–4a, 36–41; 1 Pet 2:20b–25; Jn 10:1–10

I Am Tiger Woods

"For this reason the Father loves me,
because I lay down my life
in order to take it up again." (John 10:17)

When golf phenomenon Tiger Woods was invited to play golf
    in the late 1990s with three other golf superstars,
    it was Tiger Woods who attracted
    the huge gallery and TV audience.
One television commercial that ran during the game
    showed a series of little boys and girls flashing onto the screen,
    one after another saying, "I am Tiger Woods."
He was their hero, their inspiration, and their model.
His performance challenged them and appealed to their imagination. When
    they swung their golf clubs, they identified with him.
In a sense they become one with him in their imaginations.

Our power to change lies in our imagination.
Information and willpower are helpful,
    but they lack the inspiration, the motivation,
    and the challenge of the imagination.
Those of you who play golf or any other sport know
    that too much information, as well as trying too hard,
    gets in the way of performance.
You lose the flow, become rigid and blocked.
But imagination brings the details together,
    releasing the inspirational energy.

In today's gospel, Jesus speaks to us in a parable.
He doesn't say, "I am Tiger Woods," but he does say,
    "I am the Good Shepherd." (John 10:11)

Parables, like advertising, appeal to our imagination,
    inspiring us and challenging us.
The facts contained in a parable or in advertising
    are far removed from reality.
The fact is that the little kids in the commercial are not Tiger Woods.
Likewise, Jesus is not in fact a shepherd but a carpenter.
But his image of a good shepherd inspires us and challenges us
    to reach out beyond our own self-interest toward others.

Parables are not instructions;
    they don't tell us what to do.
In his parables, Jesus doesn't give us advice
    but rather he offers us wisdom and inspiration.
They challenge a Pharisee who despises publicans,
    or a Jew who has little respect for Samaritans,
    to reach out beyond themselves.
Parables will often use negative language and logic.
They show us that the way we see the world is not true.

In his parables Jesus enables us to see the truth for ourselves.
When we see for ourselves, then we are truly free.
His parables are profoundly respectful.
He presents his reality, then allows us to compare it with our own
    and to freely choose for ourselves.
We might begin by changing his statement into a personal question.
Am I a good shepherd or just a hired hand?
Am I doing what I am doing freely
    or am I in it for the money, the power, the prestige?
Am I a good parent, partner, doctor, lawyer, secretary,
    nurse, salesperson, mechanic, priest?
Am I willing to lay down my life for those in my care?
Or do I take off when things get tough?

Tiger Woods doesn't tell these kids what to do:
    he does it, and they are inspired to do the same.
So it is with today's parable.

Jesus does not tell us what to do today: he does it.
He lays down his life for us.
He is the Good Shepherd.

We can be challenged by people like Cardinal Joseph Bernadin.
In the last years of his life,
>   he would come to the clinic for cancer treatment,
>   as did the other patients who were suffering with cancer,
>   and he would minister to them as their pastor,
>   not as a cardinal or archbishop.
He would greet them and console them with a few words,
>   and was known to write many letters to them later.
Their bond became suffering and grief.
He was a Christ figure for all of us.
We say to ourselves,
>   "I want to be like that."

In this liturgy, let us open our imaginations
>   to the challenge presented by Jesus in this parable.
Little by little, as happens in the parable of the mustard seed,
>   we will be making choices and growing to greatness.

Help us, Lord, to freely lay down our lives this week
>   for those who are committed to our care.

Acts: 9:26–31; 1 Jn 3:1–2; Jn 10:11–18

Jesus, Our Vine of Life

Frederico Fellini's film, *La Dolce Vita*,
    is hailed by critics as one of the most important films ever made.
As the film opens, viewers see a helicopter
    towing a statue of Jesus across the Italian sky.
Soon, a second helicopter appears
    carrying a writer named Marcello.
Marcello longed for more excitement
    than his rural beginnings could offer.
When he moved to the city
    in search of the life he dreamed of, however,
    Marcello eventually lost his faith.
His hopes of fulfillment dissipated into emptiness.
As the film ends, Marcello is alone on the beach,
    pondering the fate of a dead fish washed upon the shore.
Cut off from the sea and its source of life, the fish had died.
Fellini left it to his viewers to make the connection
    between the decaying fish and the empty, faithless Marcello.

Although Jesus chose other symbols
    to tell the story of humankind's need for and dependence on God,
        his point is also troubling.
Like the fish on the shore and like Marcello without his faith,
    those who separate themselves from Christ
    will be like branches cut off from the vine; they wither and die.
Those, however, who remain firmly united to the vine, who is Christ,
    will thrive and bear fruit in abundance.

In the middle of Brussels
    is the Cathedral of St. Michael and St. Gudule.

It dates back to the thirteenth century.
The altar on which the Eucharist is celebrated today
    is a remarkable one.
The surface of the altar is glass, supported by two pelicans,
    one with closed wings, the other with its wings wide open.
The pelican has traditionally been regarded
    as a symbol of parental sacrifice.
It has also been adopted by Christians to symbolize
    the sacrifice of Christ on the cross.
In the Brussels Cathedral altar, the pelican with the closed wings
    represents the contemplative, praying Church,
    and the pelican with the open wings
    is the active, outreaching Church.
Both elements, contemplative prayer and outreach,
    were integral parts of Christ's life.

How often he went away on his own to pray!
He took the disciples away to quiet places.

Religious orders reflect the dual function
    of prayer and good works.
But we are in danger if we focus too much on prayer or good works. We actually
mutilate the Body of Christ
    when we obsess on one or the other.
Jesus wrote no book and built no church building.
He entrusted his message to his friends.
He assured them that he would always be with them.
Their strength would be in their unity
    and their unity would be centered on him.
Things haven't changed.
Our very survival today depends on that unity
    both as individuals and as communities.

Why should I go to church?
Can't I meet God on my own?
Jesus was very emphatic on that point:
    "I am the vine, you are the branches." (John 15:5)

The vine and the branches are one.
To say, "I will follow Christ
    but I don't want to be part of the Church,"
    is to separate Christ from the Church,
       to cut the branches from the vine.

The altar at the Cathedral in Brussels is rich in symbolism.
The people of that bustling, busy city gather around the altar
    to be united to Christ,
    to be joined in community and communion,
       (not democracy, but community)
    to be nourished by word and Eucharist,
    to go out empowered.
There is no such thing as a solitary Christian.
United with Christ, we can do anything.
Separated from him, we can do nothing.

Today, our liturgy together,
    is an image of the vine and the branches.
The vine is Jesus and the wine is Jesus.
Wine and bread, the sign of the love we share
    and the life we seek together.

Acts 10:25–26, 34–35, 44–48; 1 Jn 4:7–10; Jn 15:9–17

I Am Only A Man Myself

On Peter's arrival Cornelius met him,
and falling at his feet, worshiped him.
But Peter made him get up, saying,
"Stand up; I am only a mortal." (Acts 10:25–26)

Archbishop Thomas Kelly of Louisville, Kentucky,
    tells a story about the day he was appointed bishop.
He made it a point to have breakfast with his mother
      on the morning the news was made public
      so that he could be with her
      when she heard the story on the radio.
When her son's appointment was announced
    during the morning news, Mrs. Kelly was thrilled.
She leaned across the table and asked,
    "What is it like for you to be made bishop?"
Kelly explained to his mother how he felt, and as he spoke,
    his mother sat with her chin on her hand, seemingly in reverie.
When he had finished, there was a pregnant pause.
Mrs. Kelly sighed and said,
    "You know, Tommy, if I had known that
    one day you would become a bishop
    and have your picture in the newspapers and on television,
    I would have had your teeth straightened."
Only a mom….

"People put me on a pedestal I don't deserve,"
    commented Billy Graham.
Another popular preacher once quoted Peter's words,
    "I am only mortal" (Acts 10:25–26)
    by saying, "I am only a man."

Not that his admirers were falling down to worship him,
    but several had remarked that
    "We come to Church when you are preaching."
Yes, they meant it as a compliment,
    and yes, we need good preaching,
    but we are only men or women.

It is fundamental for a Christian to realize
    that his or her faith is basically a relationship with Jesus Christ
    and not with the pope, with the church, or with the priest.
It is a relationship to Jesus,
    the suffering and resurrected Christ,
    the teacher and the healer.
Jesus is the one who is alive in the world today.
Jesus has to become central to one's life and faith.

How do we "make contact," so to speak, with this Christ?
We establish a relationship through word, sacrament, and people,
    especially through the people
    who make up the community of believers, the Church.
It may be occasioned by a single line from Scripture,
    or a homily such as the four words that
    Jesus spoke to his disciples: "You are my friends...." (John 15:14)
Take these words deeply into your heart and mind.

"You are my friends if you do what I command,"
    Jesus says in today's gospel (John 15:14).
Friendship has been called the most necessary form of love.
This may seem odd at first.
Surely the love of man and woman,
    the very foundation of the family and new life,
    is more fundamental.
Yes, but life goes on when we lose each other to death—
    or as believers would put it, in the return to God.

In the last passage of our lives we may find ourselves alone
      and very much in need of friends.
In institutions,
      especially hospitals, nursing homes, or retirement centers,
      a person should never be thought of as a customer or number.
(It is common language to call it the "nursing home industry.")
People who are called to the noble vocation of caregiver,
      in whatever capacity, are called to be friends. (Managed care?!)
This implies being compassionate and caring friends
      to the people to whom they are privileged to minister.
The lack of this friendship, or intimacy with anyone, can be terrible.

How many people died in Chicago's great heat wave of 1995
      because no one really knew them
      or thought to inquire about them?
Those 500 people living in their tiny rooms,
      afraid to go out or even to open the window,
      suffocated and died from the heat.
Their death was a terrible judgment on people like us
      whom Jesus told to love our neighbor.

Cardinal Joseph Bernadin,
      the beloved "Brother Joseph" of Chicago,
      was cherished as he ministered to fellow sufferers of cancer
      before he died.
Even though he was in great pain himself,
      he became their friend.
Let us strive to be like him:
      friends of Jesus, and friends of each other.

Acts 1:1–11; Eph 4:1–13; Mk 16:15–20

Heavenly Liturgy

"Men of Galilee, why do you stand looking up toward heaven?" (Acts 1:11)

For thirty-nine years I have preached,
    "Stop looking at the sky, and look around you."
But today is a day for looking upward, for looking at the sky.
What we see is not totally different from what we imagined as a child.
Today the heavens are opened.
Christ ascends, and we stand and wonder.
In fact every time we gather for Mass, Christ ascends.
Every time we offer the Body of Christ to the Father,
    the heavens are opened, the people of heaven are present,
    and the Father receives our offering.
The heavens are ruptured, and it is as if heaven and earth are one.

When God and the heavenly community look down on us
    both communities have come together to celebrate the sacraments.
That is what the Ascension is all about.
We are used to thinking of Mass in terms of the Lord's Supper,
    the sacrifice of Calvary, and the resurrection.
Today we remember that it is also about Christ soaring to the Father,
    rupturing the heavens.
Today when we offer the Body of Christ,
    yet again the heavens open
    and it is we who enter them to participate in the heavenly liturgy.

The Ascension is our feast day as we anticipate in the sacrament
    what will one day be ours in reality.
The early Christians had no difficulty with the Ascension.
For them it was vital in their celebration of Eucharist.

Conscious that the heavens were opened,
    and that they were participating in the heavenly liturgy,
    they gave us prayers that we still say today.
"And so with all the choirs of angels in heaven we proclaim,
    and join in their unending hymn of praise:
        Holy, holy, holy Lord...."

It is interesting that in our first reading
    that tension is part of Christianity,
    a tension between the "looking up" at the wonder of God
    and the "looking out" at other people and the world.
We live in a tension between prayer and good works.
Looking upward in our Sunday liturgy
    should inspire us in our gospel living.
But yet today we see many people looking down at the ground,
    burdened and depressed perhaps,
    with little sense of wonder and awe on their faces,
        little sense of joy.

Perhaps we need to look up
    so that the mystery of what we celebrate
    with our heavenly community each Sunday
    would encourage us on Monday and every other day of the week
    to go out and look for those who truly need us.

The real question today is not: "Where did Jesus go?"
What we must really contemplate is:
    "Where is Jesus asking us to go?"

Acts 2:1–11; Rom 8:6–17; Jn 14:14–16

Discovering Fire

"Come, Holy Spirit, fill the hearts of the faithful
    and enkindle in them the fire of your love.
Lord, send out your spirit,
    and renew the face of the earth."

"The day will come," said Teilhard DeChardin,
    "when after harnessing space, the winds, the tides, and gravitation,
    we shall harness for God the energies of love.
And on that day,
    for the second time in the history of the world,
    we shall have discovered fire."

Pentecost is an opportunity placed in the path of believers
    for discovering the fire that is God's love.
God is ours;
    God has been given to us as gift without reserve.
The name of this gift is Holy Spirit.
The experience of this gift is fire—
    fire in our hearts,
    fire in our bellies.
This gift is also wind and breath, so powerful as to give new life.

The love of God
    has been poured into our hearts by this Spirit
    and is living in us.
We know this gift is ours
    but we have yet to fully discover it, harness it,
    and become active participants in renewing the face of the earth.

Hans Kung, who wrote a book called *Why I Am Still a Christian*,
    suggests that as an occasional or annual plea
    "Come, Holy Spirit" is not sufficient.
Tending the fire and grasping the wind of the Spirit
    requires daily effort, struggle, and commitment.
Before the power of the Spirit can truly take hold,
    all contrary spirits must be exorcised.
Go out, you unholy spirit.
Go out, you who separate, divide, and delay.
Go out of our hearts,
    and make room for the Holy Spirit,
    who is both tender and strong,
    who reconciles and unites.

Come, Spirit of God,
    who is effective and seizes hold of us but cannot be seized,
    who gives but cannot be owned,
    who creates life and also directs.
The Holy Spirit cannot be compelled to come;
    we can only ask.

There is an attempt to describe the Holy Spirit in today's readings.
In the first reading, Luke describes
    the indescribable power of the Holy Spirit
    in terms of noise,
        like a driving wind and tongues of fire.
John's gospel speaks in terms
    of peace, truth, and forgiveness.
Paul's second reading tells of the vitality of the spirit
    bestowing a variety of different gifts
    for the sake of the common good.
Luke, Paul, and John each invite us to be seized,
    filled and on fire with the Spirit of God.

Let us close with lines by the Mexican poet and mystic, Amado Nervo. In simple imagery, he says,

Alone we are only a spark.
    but in the Spirit we are a fire.

Alone we are only a string,
    but in the Spirit we are a lyre.

Alone we are only an anthill,
    but in the Spirit we are a mountain.

Alone we are only a drop,
    but in the Spirit we are a fountain.

Alone we are only a feather,
    but in the Spirit we are wing.

Alone we are only a beggar,
    but in the Spirit we are a king.

A Glimpse of Fr. Hayes

Fr. Hayes met many celebrities in his lifetime. Early in his priesthood, he was assigned to Blessed Sacrament Church in Hibbing, Minnesota, across the street from Bob Dylan's childhood home.

He came to know Dylan quite well and was referred to in Dylan's first biography. Mike was quite proud of that, but the book was too bulky to carry around so he just neatly tore out the page that gave him a bit of fame and tucked it into his Dylan file for future reference. He particularly liked to pull it out to impress unsuspecting young adults.

— Kathleen Groh

Acts 2:1–11; 1 Cor 12:3b–7,12; Jn 20:19–23

Incomprehensible, Mysterious, Unfathomable

Most preachers shudder at the approach of Holy Trinity Sunday
    because it means we have to stand before you,
    and make comprehensible the incomprehensible,
    reasonably explain the ultimately mysterious,
    and attempt to fathom the unfathomable.
And we must do this in about ten minutes!
There is no way that I can do this.
In fact, I will not even try.
Instead of an explanation,
    the emphasis of this homily will be on application.

Thomas Edison, the inventor, once remarked:
    "We don't know what water is.
    We don't know what light is.
    We don't know what electricity is.
    We don't know what heat is.
    We have a lot of hypotheses about these things, but that is all.
    But we don't let our ignorance about these things deprive us of their use."

The truth of that statement is real.
Most of us do not know how an electric light works,
    how a telephone or television works,
    but that does not prevent us from using them.
I want to try to apply the same common sense
    to the doctrine of the Trinity.
The Trinity is not a problem to be solved.
It is not a riddle to be explained.
It is a life to be lived, and that is within reach of all of us.

God is Trinity, so God is not an aloneness.
The very essence of God is a self-giving
    and a loving relationship of persons.

God is lover (Father);
God is beloved (Son);
God is love (Holy Spirit).
We can't hope to understand and encompass
    the God who is complete love,
    but we can be in awe and worship.
God is a community of persons,
    and since we are made in the image of God,
    community and relationships are the most important things in human life.
Community and relationships influence us in every facet of our lives.
In fact, we cannot be or live without being in relationships.
Our most contented moments are always associated with times
    when we are being generous and concerned about others.

As we go through life's experiences,
    we come to see more clearly
    that loving is at the heart of being human.
The failures that pain us the most are our failures in love.
The best happiness in our lives
    comes from the love we give and receive.
Our awareness of the mystery of God
    is not simply private and personal.

The passage today from Matthew's Gospel reminds us
    that we who follow Jesus
    are bonded to him and to each other by our baptism,
    in the name of the Father, the Son and the Holy Spirit—
    in the name of a God who is love.
Little surprise that the commandment of Jesus
    is a commandment to love.
As I said, our words can't describe or contain God,
    but God does reveal his life as love.

God has given us a word for himself.
Jesus is the Word made flesh,
    the full "description" of God in human form.

As we strive to follow Jesus,
    of necessity we have to become
    more open, more aware of others, and more loving.
In so doing, we become more like God
    in whose image we are made.
The feast of the Trinity is not supposed to confuse us
    with theology we cannot understand;
    it is designed to comfort us,
    to help us realize that God comes to us
    in different ways and modes and experiences.
Celebrate God's intimate love for us,
    and you will celebrate worthily the feast of the Trinity.

And now, before I start trying to explain the Trinity,
    let us conclude together with the trinitarian action
    that has become the trademark of our faith:
        the Sign of the Cross.
In the name of the Father
    and of the Son
    and of the Holy Spirit.

A Glimpse of Fr. Hayes

Fr. Hayes was an able leader and a savvy businessman. He consolidated the Barnum, Split Rock, and Moose Lake parishes, and he oversaw the construction of Holy Angels Church in Moose Lake, Minnesota. In this day and age, it is not often that a priest would be involved in buying land and building a new church from scratch.

Of course, Fr. Hayes, a long time golfer, said that he wanted to assemble the new church structure on a golf course in Moose Lake. His tongue-in-cheek proposal was happily reversed by the church building committee.

— Dr. John Connolly, Cloquet, MN

Exodus 24:3–8; Heb 9:11–15; Mk 14:12–16, 22–26

Our Memory Gives Us Hope

I read some guidelines for preachers recently—
    or rather, a set of negatives to the preacher.
Here's a sampling:

1. Don't dwell on past glories.
Processions, expositions, incense,
    outdoor stations, forty hours devotion—
    yes, these still have an honored place in Catholic tradition
    and are still much observed in parts of Europe.
But if you refer to these,
    younger people would wonder what you are talking about
    and the homily would become a history lesson.

2. Explain transubstantiation if you wish,
    but don't get bogged down here.
Recall the warning of Monica Hellwig, a fine theologian:
    "Beginning with the Middle Ages,
        more attention was given to how Christ is present in the bread
        than to the more fundamental question, or challenge,
        of how Christ is present in us."

So today, let us dwell on the words of Jesus:
    "This is my body, which will be given for you….
    This is my blood which will be shed for you….
    Do this in memory of me."
Given and shed for you in memory of me.
Memory is about the past,
    but memory is part of the present.

A person with a badly impaired memory has no true life.
He or she can't remember what happened two minutes ago.
He or she can't keep track of conversations or time.
He or she can't keep contact with people.
Infants are bonded to parents through memory.
Memory makes us who we are.
It influences how we think and act.
It makes it possible to love.

We love this person today only because
    we remember him or her from yesterday.
Memory also makes it possible to have faith.
We believe only if we remember.
As Marty Haugen writes in one of his songs,
    "We remember, we celebrate, we believe."
That is why in the first reading,
    Moses went to so much trouble to impress his people.
He wanted them to remember.
And Israel remembered.
Their faith and their identity was defined by this memory.
Their oral and written memories
    have given us the Hebrew Testaments.

In our most intense moments of remembering,
    we often feel a presence, and closeness to someone we love.
Even when we don't feel it intensely,
    Christ is really present in the Eucharist.
His body is given to us.
His blood is poured out for us.
In our hands at this Eucharist
    is the real presence of Christ,
    in his act of perfect thanks to the Father.
We remember and join ourselves
    to his thanksgiving
    and his worship of the Father.

Being at Mass can be strange.

Our minds easily wander.

Readings, or the homily go past us.

We think about baseball or problems;

> we daydream;

> we feel restless;

> we cough;

> we get distracted.

But we came, and our coming gives us hope.

We came to remember and to give thanks.

We may do it poorly, but it is the best thing we do.

For we don't do it alone: we do it with Christ.

We remember and we discover we are one family.

We are brothers and sisters, members of the body of Christ.

At each Mass, with and through Christ,

> we worship the Father.

From each Mass,

> we go out to love and serve each other better.

On Corpus Christi Sunday

> the feast of the Body and Blood of Christ,

> I would like to finish on a high note (or a birdie or an eagle).

In 1980, there was a religious persecution in Guatemala

> that left a vast section of the country without priests.

Even though there were no priests

> to celebrate the Eucharist with them,

Guatemalan Catholics continued to meet in their churches on Sunday.

These priestless meetings are described in Fernando Bermúdez's book

> *Death and Resurrection in Guatemala.*

All present confess their sins together, aloud,

> everyone kneeling at once.

They then sing a song asking God's forgiveness.

Then a lay reader reads a passage from the Bible

> and explains it as best he or she can.

Now all are invited to share with the group

> what meaning the passage holds for them personally.

Once a month, the parishes send delegates
    to a part of Guatemala where priests still function.
Traveling as much as eighteen hours on foot,
    the delegates celebrate the Lord's Supper
    in the name of his or her parish.
The book describes one of these Masses:
The altar was covered with baskets of bread.
After the Mass each participant came up
    to take his or her basket home again.
Now the bread was Holy Communion
    for the brothers and sisters of each community.

The Catholics of Guatemala remembered and loved.
It's that kind of love for the Body of Christ that today's feast,
    the feast of the Body and Blood of Christ,
    has in mind.
Keep in mind,
    the First Supper was celebrated at Emmaus.
That is the first meal the risen Christ shared with his followers.
The feast has gone on ever since.

Ordinary Time

1 Sam 3:3b–10, 191; Cor 6:13c–15a, 17–20; Jn 1:35–42

Samuel, You've Got Mail

Nowadays, we spend a lot of time receiving information.
People can contact us in many new ways.
At the time of Samuel, the only way to call us
    was to say our name out loud.
But no longer.
We have
    voice mail,
    e-mail,
    pagers,
    cell phones,
    fax machines, and more.
Soon people will have to use larger business cards
    just to hold all the numbers used for ways to contact us!
We have a lot of information,
    but not enough time to process it.

"Too much information running through my brain!"
These words, from the song, "Too Much Information,"
    by the group, the Police,
    were written even before the Internet existed.
But there is no turning back.
Like any other technology of the last thousand years,
    it is how we use it that makes the difference.
There are no U-turns as we roar down the information highway;
    no speed limits posted and very few exits.

I once observed a couple while I was having lunch in a restaurant.
They spent more time during lunch
    checking their voice mail and talking on their cell phones
    than they did talking to each other!

We have a plethora of communication toys.
We wonder:
Is there anyone out there listening?
Is anyone home?
Are all the circuits busy?
Samuel, you've got mail.

Our Scripture lesson today deals with the story
of God's call to the young boy, Samuel.
It is a direct conversation, a startling conversation!
It changed the boy's life forever.
Samuel, whose name means "the one who listens,"
learned to do just that.
Samuel learned to listen as he lay in bed at night.
He was still and quiet.

Some of us are never still, never quiet.
The heresy of action has ex-communicated us.
We surround ourselves with sounds all the time—
when we crank the car, we turn on the radio,
when we enter our home, we turn on the TV,
and some of us cannot even sleep without the radio!
"Mea culpa" to all three for me!
When are we still and quiet?

Samuel, "the one who listens," answers,
"Speak, Lord, for your servant is listening." (1 Samuel 3:10)
It is rather dangerous to say words like that.
Why?
Because our words should turn into deeds.

"Come and see!" (John 1:39)
This is the call of Jesus.
This call will make a difference.
He is inviting us on a journey, not to a holy place,
but to a person, himself.

"Come and see" to discover your vocation
    and your "calling," whether it is high profile or not.
When we feel ill-prepared or unequal
    to the challenge of God's call,
        we are to remember that no call ever comes
            without the guarantee of grace.
When calls from God seem to conflict with our personal aspiration,
    or appears to be a detour from the course
        we have set for ourselves,
    we are challenged to renew our trust and surrender.
"Here I am for you called me." (1 Samuel 3:8)

Most of all, we are to remember
    that our God is a God of many surprises and multiple voices.
Therefore, we must be open and willing
    to hear and to heed the call of God
    from wherever, in whomever,
    and whenever it may come.

Lord, I promise that when you call,
    I will not interrupt you with call waiting!

Jon 3:1–5, 101; Cor 7:29–31; Mk 1:14–20

The King of Hearts

"Follow me and I will make you fish for people." And immediately they left their nets and followed him. (Mark 1:17–18)

The disciples made a huge gamble when they chose to follow Jesus—
    but then again, we are all gamblers.
Overcome by pity for a derelict,
    the parish priest pressed a $5.00 bill into his hand
    and whispered, "Godspeed."
Several hours later, the stranger burst into the priest's office
    and with obvious delight,
    threw a fistful of dollar bills on the priest's desk.
"Father," he exclaimed, "Godspeed paid 14-to-1 at the track!"

We are all gamblers whether we realize it or not.
We may even have a strong moral objection to gambling with money,
    but we gamble all the time with more precious stakes.
When you fall in love, you gamble.
When you decide to have a child, you gamble.
Even scientists gamble; odds are often against their research.
We are all gamblers.

To gamble means to take a chance.
Someone once said that people should not get married on Sunday
    because it's not right to gamble on a holy day!
Taking chances is what opens the door of blessing for us.
Columbus sailed west across the Atlantic for Spain
    because he bet his life on the belief that the world was round.
We owe so much to those who risked so much.

The greatest risk-taker of them all was Jesus Christ.
He laid his life on the wood of the cross and took the chance
    that we would accept the offer he made to us from that cross.
He gambled away his life in order that we might begin to realize
    money can't buy what his blood has bought for us.
Money will buy a house, but not a home;
    luxury, but not joy and happiness;
    companions, but not real friends;
    loyalty, but not love;
    medicine, but not health;
    glasses, but not vision;
    books, but not brains;
    knowledge, but not wisdom;
    a church, but not salvation;
    a bed, but not sleep;
    insurance, but not security;
    clothing, but not beauty;
    food, but not an appetite.
Money can buy a crucifix, but not salvation.

Jesus Christ took a risk
    when he made God's face visible to us from the cross.
He gambled that we would not turn our backs to him,
    thereby making his sacrifice a lost bet.
When we decide for Christ, we gamble.
We bet on honesty to win over dishonesty,
    on kindness to prevail over cruelty,
    on justice to defeat injustice,
    on peace to conquer our wars,
    on concern to triumph over hatred.
We bet on faith to overcome despair.
The Roman soldiers threw dice at the foot of the cross
    for a few pieces of clothing.
And Christ above them on the cross
    gambled for the hearts of humankind.
He was the ultimate "king of hearts."
And now it is our turn to gamble.

We are as important as the things on which we bet our lives.
So place your bets carefully;
    the day of decision has dawned.
"The time is fulfilled, and the kingdom of God has come near;
    repent, and believe in the good news." (Mark 1:15)
Place your bet at the foot of Christ's cross,
    leaving your sins there.

Maybe we need to receive the sacrament of reconciliation
    early in Lent this year,
    and hear that ageless, deathless cry:
    "Father, forgive them;
    for they know not what they are doing." (Luke 23:34)

Deut 18:15–20; 1 Cor 7:32–35; Mk 1:21–28

Holiness in the Huddle

It is Sunday, the Sabbath, a day of rest.
But this is also Super Bowl Sunday,
    the high holy day for legions of armchair athletes,
    the most sacred sporting event
    of a nationwide army of football fans.
Are you ready for some football?!
The National Football Conference
    and the American Football Conference
    will hurl their most valiant warriors at each other
    in an orgy of hitting, kicking, running, tackling,
    passing, catching, punting, and praising God.
Wait a minute: "Praising God?!"
No way!
Yes, way.

Consider this: a Jacksonville Jaguars quarterback
    informs a sideline reporter
    that God is responsible for the "Jags'" victory.
Not coaches, owners, recruiters, or trainers.
No, God is responsible.
And how does the quarterback account for the team's success?
"Thanks be to God."
There's a lot of guys on this team who really love the Lord.
When the University of Oklahoma beat archrival Texas in overtime,
    the Oklahoma coach declared on television,
    "This was Jesus Christ working through my players."
Say what?
You mean the Lord Jesus turned his back on Texas?
That God's ears were tuned only
    to the pious petitions of the people of Oklahoma?

When asked whether God would favor one side or the other
    in a match up of passionately religious players,
    coach Bill Parcells replied judiciously,
"No disrespect to anyone, but it usually works better
    when the players are good and fast."
That makes sense.

There's a lot of holiness in the huddle these days,
    how about a little more hitting and a little less preaching!
Personally I'm all for the separation of Church and football.
But this is really nothing new and not unique to the NFL.
    Steve Jones, a PGA golfer, claims to have the Lord on his side, too.
In today's gospel, there is another huddle
    and it takes place in the synagogue in Capernaum.
Jesus is providing the game plan for his players.
Suddenly, a psychotic stranger jumps on the playing field,
    a possessed, raving fan,
    a fanatic frothing like a Cleveland Brown's dawg.
Getting right in Jesus' face, he screeches,
    "What have you to do with us, Jesus of Nazareth?
    Have you come to destroy us?
    I know who you are, the Holy One of God." (Mark 1:24).

Jesus reprimands and rebukes the demon saying,
    "Be silent, and come out of him!" (Mark 1:25)
And the unclean spirit, convulsing the man and crying in a loud voice,
    comes popping out like a fumbled football.
Jesus exudes such authority that even demons obey instantly.
Jesus is pumped up with such power that even unclean spirits
    know that his arrival on the field marks the end
    of their season of domination over men and women.
There was chaos in the synagogue.
A man staggers into the synagogue like a streaker running across midfield.
Jesus takes control.
In the center of the huddle, Jesus calls the play.
It will be a two-point conversion
    designed to give victory to this demented fan.

Point one: "Be silent!" (Mark 1:25)

Point two: "Come out of him!" (Mark 1:25)

This is solid strategy for any player, on or off the field.

A conversion is a life-changing and game-winning event.

And whether you are talking about the conversion

    that first made you a disciple of Jesus Christ,

    or about a later conversion that called you

        to re-order your priorities,

    you probably need to do two things.

First: Be silent. Listen to the authoritative voice of God.

Second: Come out of him or her.

That is a call to break free, to let go, to get rid of something.

Something has got to give if we are going to go

    where Jesus wants us to go.

By the way, that's heaven—not the Super Bowl!

Praise God! Thank the Lord!

(By the way, this homily is not subject to instant replay.)

A Glimpse of Fr. Hayes

Father Hayes was never one to start Mass on time. It was one Sunday at the 8:00 AM Mass and a week before the Super Bowl. I had a lot of preparation to do for a Super Bowl party on the following Sunday, and so I put a little note in the collection plate that read: "If you start Mass on time on Super Bowl Sunday, I'll stick another five dollar bill in the collection."

On Super Bowl Sunday, Fr. Mike started Mass right at 8:00 AM. Two of our sons were altar servers that Sunday. When he got to the front of the altar, he reached in his pocket and pulled out the note and read it to the congregation. He said, "Whoever wrote this note owes me five dollars." The congregation just roared! He handed the note to one of my sons and said, "Do you recognize this handwriting?"

And so, on that Super Bowl Sunday, I put the five dollar bill in the collection with a note attached that said, "Thank you."

— Mary Kruse,
Parishioner of Holy Angels Church, Moose Lake, MN

Job 7:1–4, 6–7; 1 Cor 9:16–19, 22–23; Mk 1:29–39

What Is That Message?

Today's gospel begins with Jesus
    returning from the synagogue to Simon's house.
The remains of Simon's house have been unearthed,
    and it is near the synagogue,
    convenient for friends to gather often for Sabbath worship.
But upon arriving, they received a surprise!
It is evident that they didn't know Simon's mother-in-law was ill.
The gospel reads,
    "…and they told him about her at once." (Mark 1:30)

Jesus heals the woman,
    and it is touching that she returns the good deed.
She prepares food and drink for him
    as any good hostess would do.
Then it turns into a mob scene.
It sounds like there are demons everywhere.
But no; there were sick people everywhere.
People at that time thought of illness, any illness,
    as the work of evil spirits.
If that seems strange to us,
    think how long physicians thought the illness of a person
    was caused by something called "humours" in the blood
    and proceeded to treat the person by bleeding him or her,
    weakening the patient even further.
The theory of humours is discarded now.
So is the way of explaining illness as demonic possession.
Now we speak of germs, viruses, genes,
    and terms like epilepsy and seizures.
But this was not so in Jesus' time.
So this was not a scary scene of demons everywhere.

It was a scene of compassion, of caring, of illness,
　　and of divine presence, communicated by this person, Jesus.
We get the idea that Jesus was finally able to go to bed because it says
"In the morning, while it was still dark,
　　he got up and went out to a deserted place,
　　and there he prayed." (Mark 1:35)
There then follows an unforgettable scene.
Jesus is seeking solitude for prayer, a "deserted place,"
　　but the people track him down,
　　and his time of being alone is over.

It has been well said that we have two human needs:
　　solitude and community.
Sometimes these needs clash, as in this scene.
And so Jesus yields his time apart, his time of prayer,
　　because there is work to be done—
　　his Father's work.
And that work, announced at his baptism, is summed up again.
Jesus reminds his disciples and us of this when he says,
　　"Let us go on to the neighboring towns,
　　so that I may proclaim the message there also;
　　for that is what I came out to do." (Mark 1:38)
What is that message?
The good news is that no matter what happens in life,
　　there is a presence, a divine presence, to sustain us.

Ordinary people in their need and insecurity
　　wanted Jesus to solve their problems and heal their sickness.
The good news meant less to them than relief
　　from the pain and anxieties of life.
Afterwards, didn't they become followers?
Did they listen to his message as well as accept the gift of healing?
Nowhere does it say that Jesus healed all the sick,
　　fed all the hungry, and raised all the dead.
Anyone who has ever been to Lourdes knows
　　that the physical healings are few
　　　　(less than eighty certified by the Church in over 100 years).

However, spiritual healing is everywhere
    and is described as an experience of faith.
In seeking after miracles,
    we are a crowd "seeking signs and wonders,"
    something that Jesus expressly rebukes.
Expelling demons is not simply a matter of throwing holy water
    and saying "Be gone, Satan,"
        in spite of whatever movie you have seen.

The good news is that the God who made us continues to love us,
    and that we have the power to love,
    to confront evil and to overcome it.
That's the good news.
We have the capacity to love:
    "Let us go on to the neighboring towns
    so that I may proclaim the message there, also;
    for that is what I came out to do." (Mark 1:38)
"For that is what I have came out to do."
Here's more good news: besides solitude and community,
    there is a third human need.
That is, we need a purpose.
You have a mission, you have a purpose,
    and you have commitment to someone besides serving yourself.

George Bernard Shaw was no great believer,
    but he put this truth in biting words when he said,
  "This is the true joy of life…
        the being thoroughly worn out
        before you are thrown on the scrapheap;
        being a force of Nature instead of a feverish, selfish little clod,
        complaining that the world will not devote itself
        to making you happy."

Lev 13:1–2, 44–46; 1 Cor 10:31—11:1; Mk 1:40–45

The Edges of the Crowd

"Beware the man whose God is in the skies."　　　　—George Bernard Shaw

What a contrast between the first reading and the gospel today!
Both readings deal with the treatment of lepers,
　　although the approaches are radically different.
In the first reading, an exclusive approach is the norm: quarantine.
Lepers are segregated from other people,
　　excluded from society,
　　banished to the margins of society,
　　stripped of their dignity—
　　　　a rejected and dejected people.

There is little reason to wonder
　　why those who suffered from the dread disease
　　that we now call Hansen's disease,
　　were referred to as "the living dead."
It was a death sentence for those who contracted this disease.
The first reading gives a sample of the purification rite
　　whereby the afflicted could be restored to the community.
Why, if leprosy is incurable?

The word "unclean," encompassed more than Hansen's disease.
Taking no chances, dermatological disorders of all sorts
　　were considered unclean, for example,
　　psoriasis, eczema, acne, boils, ulcers, rashes, and even dandruff.
Unlike leprosy, many of these conditions were curable,
　　and those were the people reinstated into the community.
"Go, show yourself to the priest." (Mark 1:44)
In the gospel, Jesus adopts an inclusive approach.
He refuses to exclude from his space the leper who speaks to him.

He is happy to touch the leper.
He wants to cure the leper and he does so.
He respects his dignity.
Jesus always looked toward the edges
    of the crowds gathered around him
    and he invites those who have been banished
    to assume a center-stage role.
Often this was much to the annoyance of the other people.
In daring to touch the untouchable, Jesus becomes the outcast,
    the one who must hide.

No, I haven't seen any lepers standing in rags
    announcing that they are "unclean."
Our "lepers" today may be those
    who stand in front of us in the grocery checkout line
        with food stamps
    or our young people who wear jewelry
        in the "wrong" places on their bodies.
You get the picture.
Today's lepers are quite aware that we resist standing near them,
    that we hope they'll choose another row to sit in,
    or that we caution our children about speaking to them.
They, and we, know well the depth to which we humans can stoop
    in our desire to distance ourselves
    from those we deem unacceptable.

There is one other facet to this story about those who are "unclean."
It may be relatively easy to identify
    who the "lepers" are for each of us.
The question is this:
    Can we identify and acknowledge
    the "unclean" place within ourselves?
Those limitations or sins that discourage or embarrass us?
Do we touch that which is "untouchable" in ourselves?
If not, there's probably little chance
    we will have compassion for the flaws of others.

We are about to enter the lenten season,
  a time to strip away our pretenses and defenses
  to discover what lies beneath the layers of accumulated "stuff."

Should we choose to look deep inside,
  we may find that place within our own unique "leprosy"
  that is still in need of healing.
Perhaps we will be prompted to approach the One
  who can touch us lovingly, and make us clean.
Perhaps, kneeling together,
  we will recognize that in our deep, secret flaws,
  we and the leper are one.
In that discovery, we might be willing to widen our circle
  to include all those we keep at arm's length,
  untouchable for whatever reason.
Perhaps, come Easter,
  may each of us, like that healed leper,
  have something worth shouting about!

A Glimpse of Fr. Hayes

*Holy Angels parish community in Moose Lake, Minnesota swells in size during the summer
months when families retreat to their lake homes.*

*Our family met Fr. Hayes when we bought our cabin in 1981. We loved coming to the sum-
mer Masses with a pew full of people and listening to his wonderful stories, some of them
about Pat and Mike, our disabled sons. Sundays were happy for us "up north in God's country." Fr. Mike always shook our hands and then he would get up in our Mike's face and say,
"You have the best name in the world." Our whole family loved him.*

—The Dennis Hron family,
Summer residents, Moose Lake, MN

Isa 43:18–19, 21–22, 24b–25; 2 Cor 1:18–22; Mk 2:18–22

Is That Your Final Answer?

Who said, "No one puts new wine into old wineskins" (Mark 2:22)?
Imagine that you have four answers and only one is correct.
    a. Moses b. John the Baptist c. Elijah d. Jesus
This is like being a contestant on the television show
    "Who Wants to Be a Millionaire?"
On that show when a contestant was not sure of the correct answer,
    he or she had three lifelines.
The "50/50 " lifeline removes two wrong answers,
    thus improving one's chances.
The "poll the audience" option allows a contestant
    to ask the audience for help with the answer.
The remaining lifeline is the "call a friend" option,
    which allows the player to phone someone for an opinion.

God has also given us three lifelines to use
    when we are not sure of our final answer.

- Lifeline one (50/50) is Scripture.
  When we want to have some wrong answers removed,
      Scripture is where we start.
  The Word of God will give us guidance,
      helping us to avoid the bad choices and make good ones.

- Lifeline two (poll the audience) is the Church.
  We can poll the community of faith for support
      when we are facing the challenges of life.
  The body of Christ is there for precisely that reason.
  It is to warn when danger lurks
      and affirm when we're exercising our gifts.

- Lifeline three (call a friend) is Jesus.
    Jesus Christ himself is our lifeline friend
        who models for us the right answers,
        and on his way to the cross,
        shows us how to live a forgiving, compassionate, and loving life,
            devoid of greed.

Jesus should be our "final answer."
Is he your final answer?

A Glimpse of Fr. Hayes

Shortly after he arrived in Carlton, Minnesota in the early 1970s, Fr. Mike started putting on Irish shows around the time of St. Patrick's Day. Mike considered St. Patrick's Day to be the mark of spring and the dawning of light after the cold, short days of a long, snowy northern winter. It was referred to as his "high holy day" by his friend and fellow Irishman, Fr. Charlie Flynn. Many times the shows were celebrated in the midst of Lent.

At first I helped Fr. Hayes put on these shows using local talent or anyone else he could talk into coming and entertaining a crowd. One night he included a fellow priest whom he introduced as an IRA man on the run, wanted for various crimes by the British occupying forces in Northern Ireland. Most of the evening went by before he revealed the truth that it was Fr. Gabriel Brennan, the singing priest from Ely, Minnesota. He would call this a bit of an Irish "lark." He began to expand his audience for these St. Patrick's Day galas. He included Bishop Paul Anderson in one of his extravaganzas, as well as the local belle, famous restaurateur, and fashionable character Charlotte Zacher, of Charlotte's Café.

During the next thirty years, Fr. Hayes presented Eamonn O'Connor, Ireland's famous comic, Celtic step dancers, and Irish music groups like The Old Triangle, The Gaels, and Willowgreen. Later, after he moved to Moose Lake, Fr. Hayes impresario star shone the brightest in the new church. He hosted singer Des Allen, a play from James B. Keane, and a traveling troupe from the famed Guthrie Theater in Minneapolis.

In 2000, he brought Frank Patterson, the great Irish tenor, to Moose Lake, in his second-to-the-last performance before Patterson died. What an evening! Frank Patterson performed two forty-five minute sets in the newly-built Holy Angels Church. The parish served an elegant dinner and dessert. It was an evening I will never forget.

—Dr. John Connolly, Cloquet, MN

Note: During the years that these homilies were written, the eighth, ninth, and tenth Sundays in Ordinary Time were not observed. Therefore, they do not appear in this book.

Ezek 17:22–24; 2 Cor 5:6–10; Mk 4:26–34

That's Not What I Told You To Do

Nothing tops a good story,
 and today we are blessed with two of them.
In the first story, the reign of God is compared
 to a seed that sprouts without the farmer's knowledge.
It is the same for us.
We go along day after day, week after week,
 and sometimes it seems as though nothing is happening.
We wonder if all our work is really worth it.
Then all of a sudden, just when we are ready to give up,
 we can look around and see
 that something we have been nourishing
 is finally starting to flower.

The second story concerns the mustard seed.
We can imagine Jesus holding up a mustard seed,
 or a number of them as he tells this story.
We give different names to the Church.
The names reveal different ways of thinking and being.
We call the Church "the people of God."
This creates a picture of a group of people guided by God.
We call the Church "the body of Christ."
This implies an arrangement of organs or functions headed by Christ.
There is nothing wrong with this ancient symbol of the body.
It comes directly from the pen of Paul himself.
But it does emphasize the structure of the Church
 even as it makes a point about its unity.
Jesus chose a different image.

Instead of order, function, and efficiency,
    he thought of life and growth.
He said, "The kingdom of God is like a mustard seed." (Mark 4:31)
From a small beginning came gigantic results.
This also tells us that we, the Church,
    should be about cultivating love.
It is difficult for us to express love
    or even to own love.
The whole idea of Christianity is simple love:
    real, honest, and personal.
But we are inhibited, almost shy.
We cover our embarrassment by calling it "charity"
    because we are so afraid of the full impact
    of even the word "love."
Again, that is too bad,
    because the whole message of the gospel is love.
The Church is commanded to spread and live that love.

Love is embodied in Scripture,
    enfleshed in Jesus, and lived in the saints.
Woe to the Church if she does not pass on that love.
Above all else,
    it is the Church's business to respond like God
    to the human need for love.
Jesus did not come to frighten us out of our wits.
Jesus did not come to give us detailed instruction for living.
He did come to show us,
    that to live fully, we must be free to love one another.
But love is risky.
All of us are afraid of getting hurt
    and we need reassurance.
That is the work of the Church.
    to show us that the risk is worthwhile,
    that love is possible,
    and that God's love makes our human love holy.

Sure, it is risky,
    but God took a chance and became human.

Why does the Church find it so hard to do?!
Because you and I, who are the Church,
    are not sufficiently human.
People like Mother Teresa
    are the exception rather than the rule.
On the day of judgment,
    all of us will have to answer for our many losses of love
        on the personal level.
But we are also accountable as the Church,
    the people of God, the body of Christ—
    as the mustard seed that must grow.
On that final day, when the Church tells God
    that it has kept the faith
    and guarded the doctrine,
    Jesus just might say,
    "That's very nice, but that's not what I told you to do."

To prevent that scenario from happening,
    we better start cultivating those mustard seeds of love.

Job 38:1, 8–11; 2 Cor 5:14–17; Mk 4:35–41

A Pericope

Theology is full of its own terms,
  and "pericope" is one of them.
It is not, as a student wrote in a quiz,
  the device a submarine pokes up
  from below the surface to look around.
A pericope is
  a choice of readings from the lectionary on a given day.
Today, for example, the committee chose two verses of Job
  to match up with the gospel.

The readings today demonstrate
  the awesome power of God over raging waters.
In the first reading God penned up the ocean waves
  as easily as we would plug our sinks.
In the gospel, Jesus subdues the storming sea
  the way a mother calms a child.
"Peace! Be still!" Then the wind ceased,
  and there was a dead calm. (Mark 4:39)

Jesus spoke, as Mark Twain said,
  with "the calm confidence of a Christian holding four aces."
He knew he had an unbeatable hand.
Beyond that, he knew he was in good hands.
This is the Jesus who was fond of saying,
"So do not be afraid;
  you are of more value than many sparrows." (Matthew 10:31)
Christ will always be there.
In times of crisis, he cares.
In times of crisis, Christ is above the storm.

Is this happy talk, escapist language?
Or is it wisdom?
Of course the answer is, "Yes, it is wisdom,"
    or I wouldn't have brought it up!

Christ was with the disciples when the storm came.
Though the storm was raging,
    he was in the boat with them
    and he is still there today.
The middle of a crisis may seem
    a strange place to find Christ.
We are more inclined to look for him in some quiet harbor—
    and he is to be found there, too.
But if we are looking for Christ
    and if we are intent on finding him
    the storm is a good place to begin the search.
Jesus is right at home in the midst of chaos.

We know he grew up in a village with a bad reputation;
    he spent much of his time with people
    who were mentally, physically, and morally ill;
    he died an ugly death.
You and I will never encounter any frightening experience
    that is unfamiliar to him.
He has seen it all, right down to the edge of that black hole,
    where God seems to have forsaken us.
He knows about storms—literally and figuratively.
That is why we can trust him
    because he has been there before
    and he will be there again for us.

"Teacher, do you not care that we are perishing?" (Mark 4:38)
Who can blame them for the question?
We have asked it ourselves and will ask it again.
When we are in a time of crisis, does God care?
That lingering doubt can't be resolved by a homily
    or a story from the Bible.

In the final analysis,
    you and I must make that discovery for ourselves.
Ultimately, it comes down to another question.
Do we care?
Do we care about other people
    whose boats are on the verge of sinking?
If we care for no one but ourselves,
    how can we ever believe that anyone else cares—even God?
The answer to that is, if we care,
    we will know the caring of God.
By the simple act of caring for others,
    we will encounter the vast caring of God.

In the story, Jesus is presented as not only in the storm,
    but beyond the storm.
"Who then is this,
    that even the wind and the sea obey him?" (Mark 4:41)
He is the same one who made the blind to see, the lame to walk,
    the same one who cleansed the leper, fed the multitudes,
    and conquered death and the grave.
In times of crisis, when hope seems to be lost,
    let us remember that Christ sailed into the dark center of a storm
    and out again, leaving a peace no one could explain.
He still does that today.

Let us close with the words of John Newton
    from the hymn "Amazing Grace":

  I once was lost, but now am found;
  Was blind, but now I see.

  Through many dangers, toils, and snares
  I have already come;
  'Tis grace hath brought me safe thus far,
  And grace will lead me home.

Wis 1:13–15; 2 Cor 8:7, 9, 13–15; Mk 5:21–24, 35–43

We Are All Wanted

Do not invite death by the error of your life,
*   or bring on destruction by the works of your hands;*
*   because God did not make death, and he does not delight*
*   in the death of the living.* (Wisdom 1:13–14)

Yes, death is a reality
    but God does not delight in death:
    God delights in life.
That delight is apparent when we consider
    how the creation around us spills over with life.
In homes and fields,
    gardens and window boxes,
    and even through concrete and asphalt,
    life is bursting out in this season of growth.
The exuberant delight of the creator goes to the extravagant.

Over 4,000 species of geraniums have been codified,
    and there exists more than 3,700 types of dogwood.
Now that is extravagant!
God's extravagance extends to us as well.
Having been made for life,
    we are asked to share our life and our love.
Faith requires it.
The Jesus that we follow had an enormous passion for life
    which he shared with the leader of the synagogue
    and his daughter, whom he returned to her parents full of life.
The only thing he asked of the people
    was to give her some food.

As Jesus was generous with life and life-giving food,
   so must we do the same.
We must focus on what gives us life in our prayers and reflection,
   and in our work and our play.

Lord, make our words
   more than feeble sounds,
   and our gifts
   more than ordinary food and drink.

May they signify to us
   the life-giving presence
   of Jesus, your Son.
                              —*The Goodness of Life*

Ezek 2:2–5; 2 Cor 12:7–10; Mk 6:1–6

Disappointment

Prophets are not without honor, except in their hometown,
   and among their own kin, and in their own house." (Mark 6:4)

Going home is a great experience.
We long for familiar sights, sounds, faces.
This is especially true when we have been away for a long time.
"Don't forget where 'ere you go that you're an Irishman."
This familiar phrase was given to those
   who were leaving Ireland for the United States.
It is reasonable to assume that Jesus had a familiar feeling
   for the small city of Nazareth, where he lived all of his life,
   before his ministry called him away.
Time and distance prevented him from going home often.

Today's gospel reading tells of one of his rare visits.
He must have been excited
   and approached the town with eager anticipation.
"They will all come to meet me…
   as I touch the green, green, grass of home"
   are words from a lovely Irish-American song.
Yet this visit must have turned into
   one of the most disappointing experiences of his life.

All of us know what it is to want something
   and be forced to settle for something less desirable.
We call that experience "disappointment,"
   and it makes up a large part of our lives.
Sometimes, it is relatively small,
   like rain when you plan to golf.

At other times it is large and earth-shattering,
    as when a military chaplain comes to the door
    to deliver a death message.

Between these two experiences lies a wide range of disappointments,
    from losing a ball game to losing a job,
    from a broken heirloom to a broken heart,
    from wanting one thing to getting something else.
This is all part of what it means to be human.
Coming home to Nazareth, Jesus wasn't looking for a parade,
    a testimonial dinner, the key to the city, or a medal.
The one thing he wanted more than anything else
    was a positive response to his cause:
    his consuming passion was the reign of God.
And what mattered most to him
    was where people stood in regard to that.
Would they give themselves to it and become part of it
    or would they not?
The general consensus was that they were not interested.

For Jesus, who was seriously committed,
    this was a bitter pill to swallow.
Deep disappointment. Bittersweet.
As I said, disappointment is part of our lives,
    and the person unprepared to deal with it
    is unprepared for life in the real world.

Jesus gave us two examples of how to deal with disappointment.
First, he accepted it. A familiar proverb came to his mind,
    "Prophets are not without honor, except in their hometown,
    and among their own kin, and in their own house." (Mark 6:4)
My guess it that Jesus recited that
    more to himself than to anyone else.
He needed to hear it to give himself perspective.
It was a reminder that life
    had not singled him out for unfair treatment.

Rejection had been the common lot of the prophets.
He stood in that proud line of prophets
    so he did not take the experience of Nazareth
    as a personal affront, but as an affirmation of his ministry.
If Jesus needed that kind of reminder,
    how much more do you and I?

When disappointment comes, we tend to say,
    "Why me, Lord?"
The question is rarely a search for an answer,
    but an opportunity to complain for self-pity.
That is the worst thing we can do.
It distorts our vision, saps our strength, and handicaps our soul.
We would serve ourselves better by asking the opposite question:
    "Why not me, Lord?"
To be disappointed is part of being human.
Dreams are shattered and hearts broken everyday.
Why should you and I expect to be the exception?

The second example is that, in dealing with disappointment,
    Jesus made the most of what was available.
"And he could do no deed of power there,
    except that he laid his hands on a few sick people
    and cured them." (Mark 6:5)
That was his approach to ministry.
If he was denied the opportunity to do a big thing,
    he did a small thing.
Unable to help the many, he helped the few.
So much of his life was like that.
He dealt with difficult circumstances
    and worked with difficult people.
He did what he could,
    and the result is nothing short of incredible.
That also meant that he never gave up
    on the people of Nazareth.
This is good practical wisdom for us.

When we have to settle for less than our hopes,
  we can make the best of that situation.
It might be fragile health.
It might be shortage of money.
It might be a disappointing marriage,
  one that was going to be the best in history.
So what now?
Take what you have and do with it what you can.
That is what Jesus did.

Amos 7:12–15; Eph 1:3–14; Mk 6:7–13

Shake Off the Dust

"If any place will not welcome you and they refuse to hear you,
as you leave, shake off the dust that is on your feet
as a testimony against them." (Mark 6:11)

Palestine is a dusty land,
    and into that dusty country Jesus sent his disciples.
He told them that when a community rejected them,
    they should stop outside the village,
    and shake the dust of that experience off their feet.
It was a symbolic action against the village
    and a healing action for the disciples.
This gives us a clue to how we should handle
    life's experiences of failure: "Shake off the dust."

First let us look at how we get dust on ourselves.
We get some dust on us just by walking through life.
It never is smooth sailing all of the way.
Life is a mixture of hills and valleys,
    ups and downs, successes and failures.
Another way we get dust on ourselves is by falling down.
Sometimes we make an awful mess of life; we fall flat on our faces.
Failure can be a shattering experience.
Sometimes we get dust on ourselves
    by sitting down in the middle of the road.
We just quit and stop trying.
It is one thing to lose the game;
    it's another thing to forfeit.
It has no place in the life of a Christian.

What does dust do?

For one thing it accumulates.

We are all familiar with this aspect of dust.

This a a perfect analogy to failure.

Dust will accumulate in the corners of your life.

If you let it, it will pile higher and higher
    until it covers and colors everything that you do.

You will begin to think of yourself as a born loser.

You can hear people say, "I can't do anything right."

That person has allowed the dust of failure
    to contaminate their life.

When we collect, and remember, and brood over our failures,
        though many of them may be insignificant,
        the weight can become crushing and destructive.

How are we to deal with the dust of failure?

The first thing we should do is learn from it.

Some people learn from failure,
    while others never recover from it.

Once you have learned whatever there is to learn from a failure,
    leave it behind.

Shake off the dust; don't carry it with you.

In his poem, "Write it on Your Heart," Ralph Waldo Emerson said:
    "Finish every day and be done with it.
    You have done what you could.
    Some blunders and absurdities no doubt crept in;
        forget them as soon as you can.
    Tomorrow is a new day;
        begin it well and serenely,
        and with too high a spirit to be encumbered
        with your old nonsense.
    This day is too good and fair.
    It is too dear with hopes and aspirations
        to waste a moment on yesterday."

The last and most important matter is, try again.

"Jesus said, 'As you leave, shake off the dust that is on your feet.'

So they went out and proclaimed that all should repent.

They cast out many demons,

 and anointed with oil many who were sick

 and cured them." (Mark 6:13)

We can translate that as:

 forget your failures and keep on going.

Our failures do not have to be fatal or final.

A Glimpse of Fr. Hayes

The bishop assigned Fr. Mike to be the parish priest for a second church, Immaculate Conception in Cromwell, MN, shortly after he arrived in Carlton, MN. Mass was celebrated in Cromwell on Saturday night after Fr. Mike had already celebrated an earlier Mass at St. Francis in Carlton.

On summer evenings I would often meet him at the truck stop in the Valley of the Otters and then ride with him to the church in Cromwell, to be the lector for the evening. It was about twenty-five miles west of Carlton. Mike would put Irish music in his tape deck, light a cigarette, turn towards me and talk the whole twenty-five mile drive out to the small village. He would spend probably only a third of the time actually watching the road, which runs pretty much on an east/west line.

As I look back on these times, the trips to Cromwell and the friendship of Fr. Hayes renewed my interest in and brought me back to the Church.

—Dr. John Connolly, Cloquet, MN

Jer 23:1–6; Eph 2:13–18; Mk 6:30–34

Unrealized Possibilities

For many were coming and going,
  and they had no leisure even to eat. (Mark 6:31)

Today's gospel reading tells of a time
  when Jesus planned a holiday for himself and his apostles.
Jesus decided that all of them needed to get away
  and rest for a few days.
Things had been happening so fast
  that there had been no time to sort them out and talk them over.
But their cherished plans were not to be.
The people had followed them on foot around the lake.
Their expected solitude was buried in a wave of needy people,
  the same people they left behind on the other shore.

Life seems to take delight in disrupting our cherished plans.
Sometimes it is something simple,
  at other times it is something serious, even soul-shattering.
But that is the reality of life.
Often our only option is how we respond:
  how do we react when our plans don't work out?
The focus of the gospel story falls on the attitude of Jesus.
The disciples were probably irritated by the crowd.
Jesus, no doubt, needed and wanted that vacation
  as much as any of his disciples.
He could easily have resented the presence of that crowd
  and their intrusion on his privacy.
"As he went ashore, he saw a great crowd;
  and he had compassion for them,
  because they were like sheep without a shepherd." (Mark 6:34)

That was the reaction of the Lord to people who got in his way.
And it all had to do with the way he saw them.
To us, they often look like a bother.
To Jesus, they looked like sheep without a shepherd:
    vulnerable, lost, confused, in need of help.

If we could look at people through the eyes of Christ,
    what do you think we would see?
First, I am sure we would see invisible burdens.
Most people do not carry their heartaches in plain view;
    they bear them quietly and bravely.
But they are there nonetheless.
The couple in the car just ahead of you
        may be a father and mother
            who are worried about their son.
The woman in the supermarket may be concerned about her health,
    anxiously awaiting the doctor's report.
That elderly man may have recently lost his wife,
    a constant companion for fifty years.
A word of instruction says:
Be kind to each person you meet,
    because everyone is having a hard time.

Second, we would also see some extenuating circumstance.
The critics of Jesus thought he was too lenient towards sinners.
For example, his defense of the woman caught in adultery,
    his compassion towards a prostitute,
    his words to the dying thief.
The difference between him and his critics was a matter of insight.
They saw nothing but the failure.
He saw the pain and the problems that played a part in that failure.
When a marriage ends in divorce,
    it would be easy for you and me to be harshly critical.
But before doing that, we would be wise to pause and consider:
    what may have taken place across the years?
Could there be a long-established pattern of abuse,
    totally unknown to the outside world?

When we witness a breakdown of character
  that leads to public shame,
  it is easy for you and me to sit in judgment.
But once again, we would be wise to pause and consider:
  no event in life is complete within itself.
There is a story behind it.
Knowing that story would not excuse the offense,
  but it well might cause us to judge less severely.

Looking at people through the eyes of Christ,
  we often see extenuating circumstances.
Looking at people through the eyes of Christ,
  we also see unrealized possibilities.
That is our attitude toward children.
We look at little ones, and think of all the things they might become.
Jesus had that attitude toward people of all ages.
He looked at a man of the Pharisees, named Nicodemus,
  and saw in him the possibility of being born from above.
He looked at a rugged fisherman, Peter,
  and saw in him the makings of a spiritual rock.
He looked at the much married woman of Samaria,
  and saw her as a witness to his cause.
Someone has said,
  "Every saint has a past, and every sinner has a future."
Jesus would heartily agree with that.

"He saw a great crowd and he had compassion for them…
  and he began to teach them many things." (Mark 6:34)
The seashore became a classroom,
  and people left there that day with a few seeds of eternal truth
   planted in their minds.

If we would look at people through his eyes,
  beyond all of their burdens and failures,
  we would see unrealized possibilities.

2 Kgs 4:42–44; Eph 4:1–6; Jn 6:1–15

Barley Bread and Pickled Fish

From some angles, the gospel story of the feeding of 5,000
    is far from a spectacular miracle story.
This was no matter of life and death.
If these people had not been fed,
    they would have survived the night,
    and made their way back home, chilled, weary, and hungry.
Life would go on as before.
Here we are confronted with the ordinary action of Jesus,
    a situation that is neither dramatic nor exciting.

In this simple tale, we hear of how Jesus
    cared about people and their physical needs.
His is a mission of nourishment.
But the real hero of this story is that little boy.
He, like all children in the gospels,
    is seen as open to the presence of Jesus.
Into Jesus' hands he entrusts his lunch.
Barley bread was the cheapest bread available
    and often considered only fit for animals.
And the rest of the meal?
To be edible at all after hours in the sun,
    the rest of the meal had to be the equivalent of pickled fish.
That is what the boy hands over.
The boy helps us to understand
    why Jesus sets children before us as models.
It is because they are open.
They are willing to try something new and they are trusting.
We may see boys and girls as nothing more
    than little bundles of energy,
    but we have no idea who or what they may become.

There is no way of knowing what God may do
    with their "five barley loaves and a couple of dried fish."

Bible scholars across the centuries have wondered
    about the real meaning of this reading.
One interpretation is that most of the people
    had brought food, but were afraid to let it be known,
    lest they would have to share it with the hungry crowd.
But when a little lad came forward and gave his lunch to Jesus
    so that it might be shared with everyone,
    his generosity shamed their selfishness
        and they began to share with one another.
Once the spirit of sharing and caring took over,
    it turned out there was food enough to spare.
In fact, there were twelve baskets left over.
Five barley loaves and a couple of dried fish
    did not seem significant when compared to the need.
But in the hands of Christ, they were more than enough.

This story tells us one thing: with God, no situation is hopeless.
That is what John was assuring the early church.
And if we will listen, he will give us the same assurance today.
The issue is not how to interpret the story, the real issue is
    what do we do when we get to the end of our rope?
What do we do when we have done the best we can
    and that is not enough?
This story answers that question.
It says,
    Rest easy, my friends.
    You do not have to do it all.
    Everything does not depend on you.

We are not suggesting that everything is going to turn out all right.
We are simply saying
    that God is a major player in the game of life.
We can count on God taking part.
See how Jesus got the disciples to take part:

"Make the people sit down." (John 6:10)
And later,
    "Gather up the fragments left over." (John 6:12)
When our resources are not enough, God will make up the difference.
Isn't it strange for us to believe in God
    without expecting some marvelous results?
To say on Sunday,
    "I believe in God, the Father Almighty"
    and then go out on Monday and not expect anything to happen?
Does that make sense?!

There is a verse in the psalms that says,
    "This is the Lord's doing, and it is marvelous in our eyes."
This is how Jesus felt about life.
The feeding of the birds, the beauty of the flowers,
    are God's doing and they are marvelous in his eyes.
The healing of the sick was God's doing.
Jesus saw the hand of God in everything.
He looked at life through different eyes
    and was always finding miracles.

    "Why, who makes much of miracles?
    As for me, I know of nothing else, but miracles." (Walt Whitman)
    "Earth is crammed with heaven and every bush aflame with God,
    But only those who see take off their shoes, the rest stand around,
    and pick blackberries." (Elizabeth Barrett Browning)

In the midst of that great crowd of people,
    Andrew, a sensitive soul, made a loving discovery:
    "There is a boy here who has five barley loaves, and two fish."
You and I need to make that same discovery in our lives,
    in our world today.

Exod 16:2–4, 12–15; Eph 4:17, 20–24; Jn 6:24–35

Expectations

You and I, for the most part, spend our time here together
 thinking of what Christ expects from us.
This is as it should be.
But today, I would like to turn the thought around
 and think for a few moments of what we can expect from Christ.

I wonder if much of the religious frustrations and failures of our day
 are not the by-product of false expectations.
Many people, it seems, have come to Christ and the Church
 in search of something that is not here,
 something that he never promised to provide.
Our gospel reading for today deals with this issue.
Jesus and his disciples had just crossed the Sea of Galilee,
 from east to west.
On the eastern shore, he had fed the five thousand.
Then many of those same people had followed him
 and found him on the western shore.

But Jesus was not flattered by their desire to be with him. He said,
"Very truly, I tell you, you are looking for me,
 not because you saw signs,
 but because you ate your fill of the loaves." (John 6:26)
In other words, they were following Jesus
 because he had given them free food.
And they were hoping he would do it again.
In fact, they may have been hoping that he would become
 their meal ticket for the rest of their lives.
They would depend on him for food;
 but we can't imagine Jesus as a co-dependent.
That expectation proved to be invalid: it did not happen.

What those people wanted and what Jesus stood ready to give them
    were not at all the same.
This was not a unique event in the experience of Jesus.
People often asked him for things
    that he either would not or could not provide.
And that is still happening today.
It raises for you and me an interesting question:
    What can we expect from our religion?
In the gospel, the primary interest of the crowd
    was food for the body
Jesus' interest was in food for the soul,
    so it wasn't long before the party was over, the fat lady had sung,
     and the people went home.

This kind of thing is still happening today.
We may as well face the truth that multitudes of people
    have become disillusioned with their Christian faith.
They are looking for something they will never find.

This has to be one of the reasons why people drop out of Church,
    and turn their time and attention to other matters.
You and I are not completely off the hook for such disappointment.
There have been times when we have been less than honest
    in our proclamation of the gospel.
We have spoken of the Christian faith in glowing terms,
    as though it were the magic solution to every problem,
    the automatic answer to every question,
    and the absolute remedy for every personal and social ill
     the world has ever known.
We have reported our experience with God
    in terms of perfect peace and complete satisfaction.
All of these things may sound good in a sermon or a testimony,
    but none of them is the total truth
    and we know it.

To be sure, there are times of comfort and truth (peace) in our faith,
    but there are also times when we, too, are disappointed.

We have waited for answers that never come.
We have worked for causes that failed.
We have searched for solutions and never found them—
    at least not yet.
To put it bluntly, we all have had those moments
    when we felt that God let us down.
We should not be embarrassed to admit that.
Read your Bible and you will find yourself
    in the presence of some great spiritual company.
Who was it that prayed from a cross,
    "My God, My God, why have you forsaken me?" (Mark 15:34)

Spiritual disappointments are a fact of life,
    and no thinking person can long avoid them.
None of us can avoid them completely.
So perhaps it would help if we would take the time
    to evaluate our expectations.
What do we want from our faith?
What can we realistically expect from Christ?

Like the people in the story, we sometimes turn to Christ
    in anticipation of that which he never promised to provide,
    or could not provide.
The people in the story expected that Jesus would make life easier. One thing we
    have no right at all to expect is an easier life.
Somehow, somewhere, we have gotten the idea
    that faith in God is supposed to solve our problems,
    reduce the necessity of struggle,
    and virtually eliminate suffering.
The thing we seem to forget is that it did not work that way for Jesus.
Faith, for Jesus, was a source of strength that enabled him
    to face up to life, and carry off a victory in the face of it.
Let me quote from a letter written by a television evangelist.

He is one of those who preach that faith will make life easier.
Indeed if you have the right kind of faith,
    your days will be blest with good health and great prosperity.

Here is part of what the evangelist wrote:
  "My little boy was killed by a car
      when he was only eight years old.
  I later learned that if I had known how to believe in God,
      the angels would have protected him
      and he might still be alive today."

My friends, that is either a sad illusion
    or a deliberate distortion of biblical faith.
I suppose you can pull out a proof text here and there
    and piece together that concept.
But the overall message of Scripture is that faith in God
    does not make life easier.
And those who expect it to work that way
    are doomed to bitter disappointment.
The second reading of Paul to the Ephesians told us to
    "…put away your former way of life, your old self,
    corrupt and deluded by its lusts,
    and be renewed in the spirit of your mind:
    clothe yourselves with the new self." (Ephesians 4:20–24)

So let's go back to our original question:
    What can we expect from a Christ whose faith led him to a cross?
    What can we expect from that Christ?
How can we ever think of him as a cosmic nursemaid
    whose chief concern is making our lives a little easier?
We had better interpret our relationship with him
    not so much in terms of comfort,
      but in terms of courage and strength.
His purpose is not to make life easy for us to handle,
    but to make us strong enough to handle life
        whatever it may bring.

Friends, if you are looking for something
    that will turn your life into a bed of roses,
      then you may as well close the New Testament.
You will not find it there.

But if you are looking for someone who can fill your life
    with purpose, with power,
    then come to Christ.
We can expect that from him.
He has promised it,
    and he can provide it for you and for me.

1 Kgs 19:4–8; Eph 4:30—5:2; Jn 6:24–35

"I've Got Things For You To Do"

If your business had failed and the IRS is calling you for an audit,
    you might begin to appreciate the feelings of Elijah,
    whom we heard about in the first reading.
His business was being a prophet
    and his efforts to turn people back to Yahweh had gotten nowhere.
Queen Jezebel had put out a contract on him, as we would say today.
So his work is undone and his life is threatened.
In his despair, his wish to die was not unlike Job,
    that famous figure of misery.
He claims that he is not any better than his ancestors.

Despair is not the opposite of hope;
    it is the absence of hope.
It comes from the Latin word *desperare*.
"Sperare" means to hope, and "desperare" is to be without hope.
"Desperate" comes from the same Latin word.
We talk about "giving up" hope.
Why do we give up hope?
There really is no concrete answer; we just give it up.
This may seem obvious to us, but to most Old Testament writers,
    hope given up is hope given up to God.
Why? Because God is inescapable.
  "Where can I go from your spirit?" the psalmist asks.
  "If I ascend to heaven, you are there;
    if I make my bed in Sheol, you are there.
  If I take the wings of the morning
    and settle at the farthest limits of the sea,
    even there your hand shall lead me,
and your right hand shall hold me fast." (Psalm 139:7–9)

God is everywhere present,
    even in the depths of despair or sin.
God is present and hears the voice
    of the one who cries out, even the one who gives up.
Even when the psalmist is forsaken by God,
    it is to God that the psalmist must speak.
"My God, my God, why have you forsaken me?" (Matthew 27:46)
Jesus shares this same Old Testament view.
In his despair,
    in the absence of God and so of hope,
    Jesus call out to God:
    "My God, my God, why have you forsaken me?" (Matthew 27:46)

Elijah's despair has a modern ring to it.
It is the kind of despair we feel
    when the work we have been called to do—
    whether it is pastoring, pollution control, or parenting—
    goes wrong in some way.
It doesn't matter any longer what we do,
    nothing will go right.
Afraid and desperate, Elijah flees into the desert.
The desert is not a place of solitude
    but of loneliness and despair.

After a day's journey into the desert,
    Elijah sits down under a broom tree and he prays for death.
His despair is not so deep that he will take his own life;
    but he asks God to
    "Take away my life,
    for I am no better than my ancestors." (1 Kings 19:4)
He acknowledges he belongs to God,
    so he doesn't contemplate suicide.
The prophet's life belongs to God.
So he prays, "Take my life." (1 Kings 19:4)
Only God can do this.
And Elijah goes to sleep.
If he cannot kill himself, he can sleep.

We know this feeling, too.
How often, when things are going badly,
    do we seek to escape them in sleep?
God came, in the form of an angel,
    who touches him and makes him get up and eat something.
Elijah eats but he falls right back to sleep.
The angel reappears and wakes Elijah again.
"Get up and eat, otherwise the journey will be too much for you."
The despairing Elijah does eat, and
        "He went in the strength of that food
        forty days and forty nights to Horeb, the Mount of God."
Obviously, this is no ordinary bread.
It gives Elijah extraordinary strength.
But the bread not only strengthens Elijah,
    it nourishes him and it gives him hope.
It opens his eyes and ears.
It opens his mind and heart, so that when God comes,
    he recognizes God.
There is not time to despair, God tells him:
    "I've got work for you to do."
It was no ordinary bread, and it is no ordinary bread
    that Jesus declares in the gospel lesson today.

Jesus declares that he is
    "the bread that comes down from heaven." (John 6:50)
He explains to the skeptical Jews that he is
    "the living bread that came down from heaven." (John 6:51)
This is a most extraordinary bread indeed,
    more extraordinary than the manna
    that the ancestors ate in the wilderness.
For though they ate the bread that God provided, they died.
"Whoever eats this bread will live forever." (John 6:51)
Jesus is "the bread of life" (John 6:48) because this bread that Jesus
    "will give for the life of the world is my flesh" (John 6:51).

The Jews remained skeptical.
How can he give his flesh for the world?
How can anyone eat it?
The answers to their questions remain a mystery,
    the mystery that is the Eucharist.
We bring our despair to the Eucharist,
    and from the Eucharist we receive
    strength and nourishment, courage and hope.

The Eucharist opens our eyes and our ears,
    our minds and our hearts,
    so we are able to recognize God when God comes to us.
God comes to us in the Eucharist,
    as he came to Elijah, with more work.
This is not a time of despair, God tells us.
    "I've got things for you to do."
It matters little that we, like Elijah,
    will not get to all those things.
It is this hope that feeds us, that we feast on
    and why we celebrate the Eucharist.

A Glimpse of Fr. Hayes

I met Fr. Mike on the first tee of the Moose Lake Golf Course. Greg Gamst, one of Father's golf-ing buddies, had invited him out to play a round of golf with us. On my way home from the course that day, I thought, "What kind of a guy is this Fr. Mike?" Over a period of several years, I found out that he was a marvelous human being. Fr. Mike became a great friend of mine.

I never will forget the day when we were on the first tee and there was a big, black cloud approaching from the west. I said, "Mike, if you do not do something about this weather, there will be no golf this evening." Mike replied, "I want you to know that I am in sales and not management."

—Lee Athey, Moose Lake, MN

Prov 9:1–6; Eph 4:30—5:2; Jn 6:51–58

There Is Nothing More To Give

An artist designed an unusual door for a church in Germany.
He divided the door into four panels.
Each panel depicts an event in the gospels
    that relates to the Mass.
They relate to Jesus' gift of himself to us
    in the form of bread and wine.

The first panel depicts
    six water jars referring to the miracle at Cana
    where Jesus changed water into wine.
"The limped water saw its God and blushed."
Sometimes modern Christians have trouble seeing
    how water can change into wine.
Early Christians had no trouble with this miracle.
They lived off the soil, and saw something similar to it
    happen each summer in their vineyards.
Grapevines drew water out of the ground,
    and with the help from the sun, changed the water into wine.
But the important thing about the miracle at Cana
    is not *how* Jesus worked it, but *why* he worked it.
Was it merely to save a young couple from the embarrassment
    of running out of wine at their wedding?
The artist who designed the door suggests
    that Jesus had a deeper reason.
Jesus wanted to prepare his disciples for the Last Supper
    when he would change wine into blood.
The second panel of the door
    shows five loaves and two fish,

referring to the miracle of the loaves and fish.
Again, some modern Christians have trouble with this miracle.
Early Christians, however, had no trouble with it.
There was something similar happening each year
    in their wheat fields.
In spring they would plant five bushels of wheat
    and by the time summer ended,
    the wheat would multiply into five hundred bushels.
But again, the important thing
    is not how Jesus worked this miracle, but why.
Was it merely out of compassion for a crowd of hungry people?
Again the artist suggests another reason.
The miracle gave Jesus a chance to tell the people
    that he would soon feed them more marvelously
        than he had just done.
"The bread that I will give for the life of the world is my flesh." (John 6:51)

The third panel shows thirteen people seated at a table,
    referring to the Last Supper.
At the Last Supper Jesus does more than change water into wine.
He changed wine into his own blood.
He does more than multiply loaves of bread,
    he changed bread into his own body.
The Word made flesh is now made bread.
You heard how the writers of John describe it in today's gospel:
    "But the one who eats this bread will live forever." (John 6:59)

The last panel shows three people seated at a table,
    referring to the Easter Supper.
Jesus ate at the Emmaus truck-stop with two of his disciples.
The artist interprets the Emmaus Supper
    as the first celebration of the Lord's Supper.
Jesus took the bread and said the blessing,
    then he broke the bread and gave it to them.
This matches what Jesus did at the Lord's Supper.
The artist's door is an excellent summary of the Lord's Supper
    as it develops in the course of the gospel.

It traces it from Cana where it was prefigured,
    to Capernaum where it was promised,
    to Jerusalem where it was instituted,
    to Emmaus where it was first celebrated.
Today, we have come together to celebrate
    Jesus' gift of himself to us as our spiritual food and drink.
The mystery of love is beyond all imagining.
Jesus gives himself so completely that there is
    nothing more for him to give.

Some time ago, divers discovered a 400-year-old Spanish ship
    buried in water off the western coast of Ireland.
This area is now known as Spanish Point.
Among the treasures found in the ship
    was a man's gold wedding ring.
Etched into the wide band of the ring
    was a hand holding a heart and these words:
        "I have nothing more to give you."
The same image and sentence could be used to describe
    what today's feast is all about.
It's Jesus saying to us:
    "I have given myself to you so totally,
    that there is nothing more to give."

A Glimpse of Fr. Hayes

One day Mike missed a short putt on number one and quickly said, "Hoover." We questioned him as to what he meant by Hoover. Mike replied, "That is the biggest dam that I can think of." When we would finish our round of golf and part, Fr. Mike would just put his cart away, put his clubs in his car, and head off for home. He never said a thing! One day as we were putting our clubs in our cars, Mike walked over to me and said, "I will see you along the way, old friend."

Two days later, Greg Gamst called me at the Ridgeview Pro Shop and told me that Fr. Mike had passed away. Now I am waiting for that time when I will again see my old friend.

— Lee Athey, Moose Lake, MN

Josh 24:1–2a, 15–17, 18b; Eph 5:21–32; Jn 6:51–58

You've Got Mail

St. Paul's letter to the Ephesians was read today.
Paul is a great letter writer and would have loved e-mail!
"You've got mail!"
Someone, somewhere wants to connect and communicate with you.
Of course, you may or may not respond.
"You've got mail" is an invitation,
    not a command.

In the three readings put before the praying assembly today,
    the first reading, the responsorial psalm, and the gospel,
    God seems to be saying,
    "You've got mail: you've been invited to a banquet."
The choice is yours.
    Will you come and eat and be satisfied?
Will you RSVP?!
Remember that some of the followers of Christ
    found this teaching too hard, and decided to abandon him.

Both invitation and choice is given through the repeated refrain,
    "Taste and see that the Lord is good." (Psalm 34:8)
The psalmist reminds us of the privilege that is ours
    if only we take the time to respond to God's invitation.
"You've got mail," God says with the gift of each new day.
"Can you discern my message in the beauty of the sunrise
    and the music of the birds?
Can you read between the lines of your daily joys,
    struggles, and sufferings and hear my voice?"
God's voice is familiar;
    after all he joined us and shared our DNA.

"You've got mail," God says on every page of Scripture,
   from Amos, Hosea, Micah, Jeremiah, Ezekiel, Isaiah,
      Paul, James, and John.
"You've got mail," God says, "and his name is Jesus.
   His saving story continues to be proclaimed.
   Are you listening and living accordingly?"
"You've got mail," God says in every sacramental moment.
   "Can you see beyond the signs and symbols
   and hear my promises of love, forgiveness, healing,
      presence, and peace?"
"You've got mail," God says,
   "Can you hear me pleading for your compassion
   through the silent screams of the unborn,
      the poor, the hungry, the thirsty, the naked, and the lost?"
"Will you listen? Do you hear?
   Will you respond?"

"Will you download my messages
   and make them a priority in your life?
Or will you take the path of least resistance and least involvement,
   pressing delete, turning a deaf ear and a hardened heart
      to my many invitations to you?"
"You've got mail," God says.

Deut 4:1–2, 6–8; Ps 15:2–3a, 3b–4a, 4b–5, Mk 7:1–8, 14–15, 21–23

Lip-Synching

"This people honors me with their lips
but their hearts are far from me;
in vain do they worship me." (Mark 7:7b)

In 1990, the group Milli Vanilli caused quite a music controversy.
The duo of Rob and Fab had exploded on the pop music scene.
They had five big hits, including three number one songs.
Then it was discovered that they weren't really singing
    on their records or at their concerts—
        they were simply lip–synching.
The actual vocals were being sung by two former American soldiers
    who just didn't have the "look" the record producer wanted.
People in the recording industry were outraged,
    and Milli Vanilli had to give back the Grammy Award
        given to them for Best New Artist.

In today's gospel, Jesus says that the Pharisees, like Milli Vanilli,
    were doing an Old Testament lip-synch.
They were mouthing the appropriate and necessary words,
    but they were not doing the hard work
    that God requires of all of us.
Jesus quoted Isaiah's prophecy
    when he spoke to the Pharisees and the Scribes saying,
    "This people honors me with their lips
    but their hearts are far from me." (Mark 7:7)
Would he say the same of us?
Let's suppose that Jesus Christ was in this church right now,
    sharing this celebration with us.
We would certainly want to show him
    that we are fully participating in the Mass.

But wait! Jesus is here with us in this place of worship right now.
If we are merely lip-synching our way through the Mass,
    we become the twenty-first century Pharisees.
We become the Milli Vanilli of the Mass.

The "lip service" the Pharisees were accused of sounds like us
    when we come to Mass out of habit,
    bringing our bodies but leaving our hearts at home.
Our challenge is to bring our hearts to Mass each and every time,
    and to pay more than lip-service to Jesus.
When we say the Creed,
    there should be no doubt that these are the things
    we believe in as Catholics.
When we say the Lord's Prayer,
    there should be no question that we give
    our praise and thanks to God,
    and that we will forgive others as we ask for forgiveness from God.
When we receive Communion,
    we should say, "Amen," and truly mean that we believe
    we are receiving the body of Jesus Christ.

  The Christian Social Union
    was very much annoyed
  because there were some evils
    we really should avoid
  and so they sang another hymn
    to help the unemployed.
                    —G.K. Chesterton

This is lip-service religion.
Chesterton was not knocking prayer, or hymn singing.
But prayer that has become a mere moving of the lips,
    when there is no change inside us, is hollow.
When there are no deeds in the world that show
    that Christians live here, we have become Milli Vanillis.

A Glimpse of Fr. Hayes

One night Fr. Hayes and a friend decided they wanted to drive two miles west of Carlton, Minnesota to have a late night snack at the truck stop. In addition, Mike decided that Brendan, his German Shepherd, needed a workout—at 1:30 in the morning. Mike drove his car slowly on the side of Highway 210. In the middle of Brendan's workout, a sheriff's patrol car flashed its light and pulled in behind Mike's vehicle.

Innocently, Mike poked his head out of the window and said, "Is there something the matter, officer?" He talked himself out of a ticket that night.

—Dr. John Connolly, Cloquet, MN

Isa 35:4–7a; Jas 1:17–18, 21b–22, 27; Mk 7:31–37

Be Opened

He had done everything well; he even makes
the deaf to hear and the mute to speak. (Mark 7:37)

Hear and speak.
"Imagine there's no heaven," sang John Lennon.
Imagine there is no cell phone!
In a society in which talking on the cell phone
    is common while driving,
    can mini-vans with washers and dryers be far behind?!
This is called multi-tasking or burning the candle at both ends—
    and in the middle.
Are we happier for this?
    Are we less prone to error in juggling so many tasks?!

In today's gospel lesson,
    Jesus applied his healing touch to a deaf man
    who also suffered from an impediment in his speech.
The miracles of Jesus are signs that to believe in him
    is to live in hope and expectation.
The deaf man with the speech impediment lived in hope
    and expectation that one day he would be able to use a cell phone.
The Gospel of Mark tells us:
    "'Ephatha,' that is, 'Be opened,'
    and immediately his ears were opened, his tongue was released,
    and he spoke plainly." (Mark 7:34)
As for the people who witnessed this miracle of healing,
    in Mark's words,
    "They were astounded beyond measure." (Mark 7:37)
Jesus performed this miracle for a man
    who really wanted to be healed.

And Jesus offers us his healing touch
    in areas of our lives that cripple us.
But there is one necessary condition:
    we really must want to be healed.
One cannot read the gospel with any kind of objectivity
    without realizing that healing was a major mission of Jesus.

In Matthew's gospel,
    there is a little summary of events that speaks of Jesus curing
    demoniacs, paralytics, epileptics, the blind and the deaf,
    those with skin diseases, and many others.
But that was only the beginning.
He intended that his disciples would be healers, too.
    "The things that I do," he said to them,
    "greater things you will be able to do."
Astonishing!

There is a well-known painting by the artist, Duccio,
    that shows Jesus reaching out to touch and heal a blind man
    and his disciples looking over his shoulder, watching.
It reminds us of a senior doctor making his rounds in the hospital
    with the young interns following along trying to determine,
        "How did he do that?"
And that says something about our ministry,
    because we are expected to learn
    how Jesus did that.
We are Jesus' healing interns in this sense.
    The miraculous gift of life we have received
     is from a gracious God.
You are a living miracle.
You are one of God's originals.
You are one of a kind.
You are necessary.
You belong.

God's plan for the fulfillment of his creation
  and the coming of his kingdom, includes you.
God needs you and we need each other.
In order to experience the miracle of God's love to the fullest,
  we need to share it with each other.
And when we do, our amazement will go beyond all bounds.
"Ephphata!" "Be opened."

Let us open our minds and hearts to the miracle of God's love
  and our weary, anxious, multi-tasking, fearful souls
    will be healed.
When we gather for Eucharist, we don't begin our ministry,
  we celebrate the ministry.
We have lived one week and prepare to live the next one.

Isa 50:4–9a; Jas 2:14–18; Mk 8:27–35

Who Do People Say That I Am?

"Who do people say that I am?" (Mark 8:27)
When Peter gave the answer, Jesus did not say,
　"It's about time you figured that out."
Jesus is preparing, not to win an election or war,
　　but to do battle with the forces of evil,
　　to give final meaning to human existence.
"Who do people say that I am?" (Mark 8:27)

　And Jesus was a sailor
　When he walked upon the water
　And he spent a long time watching
　From the lonely wooden tower.

　And when he knew for certain,
　Only drowning men could see him
　He said all men will be sailors then
　Until the sea shall free them.
　　　　　　　— Leonard Cohen, "Suzanne"

"Who do people say that I am?"
Who am I, really? Who are you, really?
The awesome reality is that each of us
　is a unique masterpiece of God's creation.
Some eighty billion of us human persons
　have come onto planet earth
　and each one of us is an eighty-billionth wonder of the world.

Genetics tell us that prior to birth,
   each person has an array of genes
   unlike that of any other person, living or dead.

Each set of fingerprints, footprints, voiceprints, is unmatched.
Heart specialists tell that no two cardiograms are alike.
Neurologists tell us that no two brainwave tests
   produce the exact same results.
We have reached a point in time when it is
   relatively easy to establish one's identity,
   and virtually impossible to conceal it.
Yet even with fingerprints, footprints, cardiograms, voiceprints,
   DNA samples, and brainwaves not withstanding,
   we never cease to ask ourselves and each other "Who am I?"
"Who do you say that I am?"

In answer to the first question, the disciples tell Jesus
   that some people identify him as John the Baptist,
   and others as Elijah and still others as simply a prophet.
But to the question, "Who do you say I am?"
   the apostle Peter gives the answer:
"You are the Messiah." (Mark 8:29)
The Messiah, the anointed one, Christos.
Jesus' question concerning his identity has nothing to do with
   fingerprints, height, weight, skin color, hair, eyes, or date of birth.
Jesus' question is not addressed to his followers' senses alone.
   How do I look? How do I sound?
   How do I feel? How do I smell?
Jesus' question is addressed to the heart,
   which, in biblical terms, means the whole person.
Jesus is asking:
   What does my life and presence mean to your life?
   What is your understanding of my mission?
   Why do you follow me wherever I go?
   Why do you listen to my preaching and teaching?
   What do I mean to you?

These are the kind of questions Jesus implies in those six little words:
    "Who do you say I am?" (Mark 8:27)
Peter sums up his perfect answer in the simple little phrase
    "You are the Christ." (Mark 8:29)
Jesus put the question to his disciples.
Knowledge is a powerful force.
Knowledge has changed the course of history.
A doctor's knowledge saves lives;
    a pilot's knowledge ensures the safe return of the traveler;
    a teacher's knowledge helps to dispel ignorance and so on.
Christ tests the knowledge of his disciples.
He did this because he knew how critical their knowledge of him
    would be for the success of their mission:
"Go and teach all nations."
"Euntes docete omnes Gentes."

We all experience Christ in different ways.
In our society, many people, especially the young,
    live beyond the threshold of the Church.
Many others do not know Christ at all, and sadly,
    there are those who have rejected Christ and the Church.
The whole Church must shoulder the responsibility
    for leading God's people, especially the young,
        to the knowledge of Christ.
The only adequate response in the face of this awesome task
    is not the new *Catechism*, but prayer.

In prayer, Christ will impart to us
    the knowledge of what to do and where to go.
For his sake and for the sake of those who do not know him,
    let us make the prayer of St. Anselm (1033–1109) our own.

   O Lord my God,
   I have not yet done that for which I was made.
   Teach me to seek you,
      for I cannot seek you unless you teach me
      or find you unless you show yourself to me.

Wis 2:12, 17–20; Jas 3:16—4:3; Mk 9:30–37

The Great Business of Living

Some years ago there was a musical comedy on Broadway
    called *How to Succeed in Business Without Really Trying*.
It was about a young man who had a job as an office boy.
He emptied the wastebaskets and did other rather menial tasks.
But by using trickery and flattery
    he got one promotion after another
    and finally ended up as CEO.
It was all done in good humor, of course.
But it was also a commentary on how our society understands success.
We might expect that kind of thinking from the world.
But today, we are in Church
    where a different set of values should prevail.

This is the time and place
    for us to reconsider the whole concept of success.
No one wants to fail.
All of us like to succeed in the great business of living.
But we need to know what that means.
You heard about the man who climbed the ladder of success
    only to discover that it was leaning against the wrong wall.
That can really happen to a person.
A friend said of Ernest Hemingway,
    "He was a success at everything except life."
My concern is that this not be true of me or of you.
Each of us has only one life to live.
We do not want to come to the end
    and discover that our ladder
    was leaning against the wrong wall.

Most of us would agree that the great expert on life is Jesus.
He knew how to live; this was his specialty.
In a few short years, he built a life
    that has made a lasting impact on the world.
What did success mean to him?
Our gospel reading tells us about a day
    when he talked on this all important subject to his disciples.
They were no less confused about what success in life meant
    than we are.
Their goal in life was to gain prominence and prestige.

A debate broke out among the disciples
    as to who was the most important among them.
No doubt, every one of them aspired to that position.
Jesus overheard that argument and told them how to settle it.
He said:
"Whoever wants to be first
    must be last of all and servant of all." (Mark 9:35)

Let me tell you a story.
An old monk prayed many years
    for a vision from God to strengthen his faith,
    but it never came.
He had almost given up hope when one day a vision appeared.
The old monk was overjoyed.
But then, right in the middle of the vision,
    the monastery bell rang.
The ringing of the bell meant it was time to feed the poor
    who gathered daily at the monastery gate.
It was the old monk's turn to feed them.
If he failed to show up with food,
    the unfortunate people would leave quietly,
    thinking the monastery had nothing to give to them that day.
The old monk was torn between his earthly duty
    and his heavenly vision.

But, before the bell stopped ringing,
    the monk made his decision.
With a heavy heart, he turned his back on the vision
    and went off to feed the poor.
Nearly an hour later, the old monk returned to his room.
When he opened the door, he could hardly believe his eyes.
There in the room was the vision, waiting for him.
As the monk dropped to his knees in thanksgiving,
    the vision said to him,
    "My son, had you not gone off to feed the poor,
    I would not have stayed."

That story bears a striking resemblance to today's gospel.
The monk, like the disciples,
    learned the most important spiritual lesson of his life.
He learned that the best way to serve God
    is not necessarily to give up everything.
He learned the best way to serve God
    is not necessarily to turn our back on the world
        and go off to a monastery.
He learned the best way to serve God
    is not necessarily to spend hours in prayer,
        contemplating heavenly visions.
The best way to serve God is to do something far more basic.
The best way to serve God is to reach out in service,
    especially to those less gifted than ourselves.

Jesus taught his disciples this lesson:
    "Whoever wants to be first must be last of all
        and be the servant of all."
Who have been the most important people in your life?
Most of them, I dare say, were neither rich nor famous.
And even if they were both rich and famous,
    those were not the things that mattered.
I can't tell you the names of the truly important people in your life,
    but I can tell you what they did.

They took care of you when you could not take care of yourself.
They taught you to read and write.
They spent time with you when you were lonely.
They corrected you when you went astray.
They encouraged you to follow the right path.
The most important people in your life
    have been those who helped you.
Those who helped you to be gentle with yourself.
In other words, they were your servants.

So the strange concept of Jesus is not so strange after all:
    the meaning of success is service.

  "I don't know what your destiny will be.
  But one thing I know,
      the only ones of you who will be really happy
      are those who sought and found how to serve."
                                    — Albert Schweitzer

Num 11:25–29; Jas 5:1–6; Mk 9:38–43, 45, 47–48

Them or Us

The Holy Spirit gathers us this Lord's Day
    to ponder difficult questions.
Who belongs to Christ and who should be excluded?
Jesus offers a straightforward answer.
"Anyone who is not against us is for us." (Mark 9:40)
Jesus' words deserve repeating.
"Anyone who is not against us is for us."
They can be hard words to live by.

Each of the readings for today's liturgy
    invited the gathered assembly to become more aware
    and appreciative of the Spirit of God at work in others,
        even those we least expect.

Both the first part of the gospel and the first reading are saying,
Look, some other people seem to have the Spirit,
    or are they speaking for God, working for God, acting as prophets,
    or confronting evil and replacing it with good?
They are not one of us so should we stop them?
This is a classic "them" or "us" scenario.
It is the old tension between the Church as a "club for saints"
    or a "hospital for sinners."
The answer from Moses and Jesus is
No! Cheer them on! They are doing God's work and God sometimes
    takes the spotlight away from us and gives it to others.
The differences between churches furnishes an example.
Because Christianity is divided into many churches,
    it has been difficult for their members
    to say good things about each other.

For many Protestants, Catholics were idol worshippers.
And Catholics considered everyone else to be heretics.
A "them" and "us" mentality:
>   had Christian churches through the centuries
>   paid more attention to today's Scripture,
>   efforts to find moral and religious common ground
>   would not have been so long in coming.

The disciples of Jesus were just like the rest of us.
They thought they had a monopoly on truth
>   so they tried to stop a man who was performing miracles
>   because he was not of their company.
Jesus replied in no uncertain terms.
>   "Anyone who is not against us is for us." (Mark 9:40)
He states the same principle even more strongly in John's gospel.
>   "I have other sheep that do not belong to this fold." (John 10:16)
Apparently Jesus did not limit his friends
>   to his close circle of followers—and neither should we.
Jesus' response is tolerance and acceptance.
He adds some important comments, such as,
>   a person does not have to do much to be on Jesus' side.
He tells us that even if a person only
>   "gives you a cup of water to drink
>   because you bear the name of Christ
>   will by no means lose the reward." (Mark 9:41)

Jesus welcomed as a friend any person
>   who does the most menial deed as an act of love.
Remember his description of the great judgment?
He numbers among his friends those who had
>   given a drink of water to the thirsty, given clothing to the naked,
>   given bread to the hungry, and given shelter to the homeless.
Simple deeds like these are ways of befriending Jesus.
Jesus said, "'Truly I tell you, just as you did it
>   to one of the least of these who are members of my family,
>   you did it to me." (Matthew 25:40)

Anyone who is a helper or a healer is a friend of Jesus.
But how can we call helpers and healers friends of Jesus
    if they do not profess his name?
It's one thing to say all Christian helpers and healers
    are friends of Jesus regardless of their denomination.
It's another thing to say that Jesus recognizes all helpers and healers
    whatever their faith or the lack of it.
How can that be?
The great Catholic theologian Karl Rahner
    speaks of "anonymous Christians,"
    those men and women who are doing the work of Christ
        without ever hearing his name.
Jesus is our friend, but like any friend,
    he wants our friendship in return.
He want us to be helpers and healers just as he is for us.

Here and in a thousand other places is your apostolic turf—
    not by papal or episcopal permission,
    not by patronage of your pastor,
    not by filling the gap and doing this work
        until we can find more men to wear Roman collars.
Here you are the Church,
    by God's gracious calling and the power of your baptism.
To paraphrase Moses' words,
    "Would that the Lord might bestow his Spirit on us all."

Gen 2:18–24; Heb 2:9–11; Mk 10:2–16 or 10:2–12

Children's Ministry

"Let the little children come to me, and do not stop them;
  for it is to such as these that the kingdom of God belongs." (Mark 10:14)

There is nothing remarkable about the fact that Jesus loved children—
  most of us love children.
But there is something significant about this particular occasion.
Jesus is on his way to Jerusalem for the last time.
He was going to die, and he knew it.
He told his disciples, but they didn't understand.
The weight of the world was on his shoulders
  and he was carrying it alone.
At a time like this, one of personal stress,
  most of us become impatient
  and have little or no time for children.
But that was the very time
  when Jesus wanted children to be around him.
He gathered them in his arms, blessed them,
  and perhaps even played with them for a while.

Jesus' love of children was obviously something more than sentiment.
It was a conscious commitment.
He cared for them and believed in them very deeply.
"It is to just such as these
  that the kingdom of God belongs." (Mark 10:14)
If you and I love children in the same sense that the Lord does,
  it will do more than give us a warm feeling inside.
For one thing it will teach us, or remind us,
  of the spirit of discovery that belongs to childhood.
Most of their sentences begin with what, where, when, why, and how.
They live in a world filled with wonder; they walk in wonderland.

Everything is new.

Who will guess what new discoveries this day will bring?

A new word learned, a new idea introduced, a new friend made—
    anything can happen.

You had better be prepared to answer the questions of children.

Listen to this wonderful dialogue between Amelia Dahl and her grandson Ricky.

Ricky: Grandma, why do trees take their clothes off at the end of summer?

Grandma: Because they get worn out and must be exchanged for new ones.

Ricky: Where do their new clothes come from?

Grandma: From underneath the ground. Deep down, mother nature is busy
              preparing a new spring wardrobe for them.

Ricky: Grandma, did you ever notice that the sky looks like an upside-
              down lake?

Grandma: And those little white clouds look like sailboats, don't they?

Ricky: I wonder where they're sailing to.

Grandma: Maybe a cloud meeting.

Ricky: What would they do there?

Grandma: Probably decide if the earth needs more rain.

Ricky: Gee, God thinks of everything, doesn't he, Grandma?

What a beautiful attitude to start life with.

We all start out life with it.

But somewhere along the way, we lose it.

We lose it because we stop searching, reaching,
    thinking, learning, and growing.

Instead of discovery, life becomes a holding pattern.

We stop reaching out and start digging in.

Instead of taking charge, we start playing it safe.

Instead of blazing trails, we start building fortresses.

Instead of thinking new thoughts, we start defending old ideas
    with which we have become comfortable.

Have you and I already become all God wants us to be?

Surely, none of us believes we have.

We all know better.

We will never outgrow the spirit of adventure
    and discovery which we once knew as children!
It belongs to all of life, and that is a reason why Jesus said,
    "Whoever does not receive the kingdom of God,
    as a little child will never enter it." (Mark 10:15)
Another thing that will happen to us,
    if you and I love children in the same sense as the Lord,
    is that it will create and sustain a spirit of hope within us.

It has been often said "the birth of a baby is a sure sign
    that God has not given up on the world."
There is no telling what will happen.
Who knows what door those tiny hands will open!
Jesus must have felt that as the children gathered around him.
He was going to Jerusalem
    where the atmosphere would be heavy with hatred.
But there, for a little while,
    he was looking into fresh faces, and feeling the love and trust
        that belongs in a special way to the young.

When you and I become discouraged about the human race
    there are a number of ways to deal with it.
We can read the Bible and be reminded
    that people always had problems,
    none of which had been too great for the grace of God.
We can pray and draw upon that divine power
    that renews the strength of the inner person.
We can visit with a friend in whom we can see
    the qualities that make life worth living.
Or we can do what Jesus did and spend a little time with children.
We think of this gospel in terms of ministry to children,
    which is certainly true.
We think of the ministry of parents and teachers of children,
    which we certainly should.
But be also sure of this, these little ones ministered to Jesus.
He needed what they had to give—
    and so do we.

Wis 7:7–11; Heb 4:12–13; Mk 10:17–30 or 10:17–27

Love Requires More

"God's Word is living and effective, sharper than any two-edged sword…
it judges the reflections and thoughts of the heart." (Hebrews 4:12)

Like the rich man in today's gospel,
    we may at times want to move ahead with our lives,
        but cannot quite do so.
Letting go of our security blanket
    is a frightening prospect.
The rich man's challenge becomes our challenge.
Like him, we are continually called to peel away
    deeper layers of the gospel message.
We, too, must put aside whatever stands between us
    and a total response to God.

Our gospel reading today presents a picture rarely seen in society—
    any society.
A rich man kneels at the feet of a poor man.
Commonly,
    it is the poor who bow to the rich occasionally in respect,
    but more often in acknowledgement that wealth is power.
The poor man we know quite well.
His name was Jesus.
The rich man is not so well-known.
The story leaves him nameless,
    but it tell us something.
When Jesus reminded him of the ethical portion of the ten commandments,
    he replied,
    "Teacher, I have kept all of these since my youth." (Mark 10:20)
The man was sincere.
Jesus accepted that at face value.

It is something to be admired.
The record says,
    "Jesus, looking at him, loved him...." (Mark 10:21)
There is tenderness in that statement.
But along with tenderness, there is also challenge.
The demands of love are always greater
    than the demands of law.
This man was soon to learn
    that it is one thing to avoid hurting others:
        the law requires that.
It is another thing to give one's self sacrificially
    for the benefit of others:
        love requires that.

When we look at our social obligations through the eyes of Christ,
    new meanings begin to appear.
They are not so simple as, at first, they may seem.
The law says, "You shall not murder." (Mark 10:19)
The rich man had kept that command.
Murder to him was unthinkable.
And so it is with you and me.
We can hardly imagine taking the life of another human being,
    let alone actually doing it.
That is a good thing.
The world would be a better and safer place
    if everyone felt that way.

But with Jesus,
    that kind of goodness was not enough.
He looked at people through the eyes of love,
and that gave the commandments a deeper dimension.
To spare the life of another human being is one thing.
To truly value the life of another person is another.
When we see people as Jesus saw them,
    we will not simply let them live;
        we will help them live.

The law of course does not require us to do that—
    but Jesus did.
With him, the ordinary kind of goodness was not good enough.
He expected more.
Consider one other word from the law,
"Honor your father and mother." (Mark 10:19)
We focus our thoughts on those who cared for us in childhood.
We owe them something, for the rest of their lives.
Most of us accept that.
That is good, but it is not good enough. Love requires more.

On an occasion Jesus said,
"Whoever does the will of God
    is my brother and sister and mother." (Mark 3:35)
With him the family attitude went beyond blood ties.
An old adage says, "Charity begins at home."
The Lord would agree with that.
Home is a proper place for charity to begin,
    but not the place for it to end.
That spirit of care, of acceptance and honor
    has no stopping place until it includes the whole human family.
The law of course does not require that—but Jesus did.
With him ordinary goodness was not good enough:
    he expected more.

Must we take the claims of Christ so seriously?
Can't we just be decent men and women?
Why wouldn't that be enough?

A writer tells this amusing story in one of his writings.
A young door-to-door salesman was assigned to a rural area.
One day he came upon a farmer
    seated in a rocking chair on his front porch.
The young man went up to the farmer enthusiastically and said,
"Sir, I have a book here that will tell you how to farm
    ten times better than you are doing now."
The farmer didn't bother to look up; he simply kept on rocking.

Finally, after a few minutes,
    he glanced up at the young salesman and said,
    "Young man, I don't need your book.
I already know how to farm ten times better than I'm doing now."
This is a good illustration of what Jesus is talking about today.
The farmer was capable of farming better
    but he lacked the commitment to do so.
The rich man was capable of doing more
    than just keeping the commandments
    but he lacked the commitment to do so.

The gospel today makes it painfully clear
    that there is more to Christianity
        than just keeping the commandments.
We can be grateful for a Christ
    who requires more of us than respectability.
Whether we ever rise to his challenge or not,
    we can be glad that he demands something more dynamic
        than mere decency.
With him, ordinary goodness is not good enough:
    he expects more.

Isa 53:10–11; Heb 5:1–6; Mk 10:35–45

Where Do You Stand?

"Grant us to sit, one at your right hand and one at your left, in your glory."
(Mark 10:37)

Where are you sitting right now?
Is it the place you usually sit when you come here?
Teachers will tell you that students like to take the same seats
 each time they come into class,
 and get upset if someone else sits in "their" desk.
If there is not an established order to things,
 kids will often fight about who gets to sit
  in the front seat of the car,
 or on the sofa instead of the chair.
It is not only children who are concerned with seating arrangements.
We adults care about where we sit at a concert, a play, or a game.
It is an honor to be seated at the head table
 at a wedding or banquet.

We probably wouldn't think to describe ourselves this way,
 but we are people who care about where we sit.
In my case, will it be a table or a booth at the diner?
James and John ask for seats
 at the right and left hand of Jesus in his glory.
When the kingdom comes
 they don't want to miss out on any of the perks.
James and John are looking for the best seats in heaven.
It helps to remember that John and James
 are described elsewhere in the gospels as "the sons of thunder."
But sharing Jesus' mission is much more demanding
 than buying a ticket or getting a reserved place at the table.

A good comparison is to the wedding.
Those at the head table are not those who promise to share
    the life of the newlyweds at some undefined point in the future,
    but those who have already shared their lives, their struggles,
       their sorrows, and their joys.
It would be a poor friend who entered a relationship
    with the goal of getting a good seat at the wedding!
That is what Jesus says to James and John.
We are to fix our eyes on God's kingdom
    with courage, compassion, faithfulness, and love
    to bring about the kingdom—
       not to gain a good seat when the kingdom comes.

When all the disciples are gathered,
    Jesus repeats the theme of true discipleship.
Turning conventional wisdom on its head, Jesus declares that
    it is only in service that one may become great.
With clarity and simplicity, Jesus says
    that anyone who serves the rest is the way to aspire to greatness.
And the more servant-like the service,
    the greater the genuine stature of the disciple.
It was modeled again at the Last Supper
    through the washing of the feet.
"For the Son of Man came not to be served but to serve,
    and to give his life as ransom for many." (Mark 10:45)

In one sense today's gospel is not about sitting at all:
    it's about standing.
Jesus tells James and John, or tries to explain to them,
    that it is not where they sit that counts
    but how, for what, and with whom they stand.
Think about last week, and some of the many places you stood:
    in a check-out line, at the front of the class, over a hot stove,
    conducting a meeting, contemplating the stars,
    at your front door responding to an unexpected knock.
How did you stand there?!

Did you stand as Jesus might have, expectantly and open?
Or did you stand as James and John,
     looking forward to something better,
     awaiting somewhere else?

This week be conscious of where and how you stand.
Stand as you would with Jesus at your side,
     thinking not "what's in it for me"
     but "what's in it for God."
That is greatness.
If you do it right
     everyone is number one
          because there is no number two.

Jer 31:7–9; Heb 9:24–28; Mk 12:28b–34

Beggars Can't Be Choosers

Today's readings are about coming to see again in a new way.
Being short-sighted, or blind to what we are doing,
   is something that most of us go through at some point in our life.
Something happens like an illness, or a broken relationship,
   and our life becomes dark.
Emotions are mixed up and what used to be clear is cloudy.
Where we used to see straight, it is now blurry.
We begin to behave in harmful ways,
   hurting ourselves and hurting others.
We begin to look for light at the end of the tunnel.

To see things differently is what lies behind the telling
   of the story of Bartimaeus, the blind man.
The Gospel of Mark tells the story for a good reason.
Jesus was on the way to Jerusalem, where he had said he would be put to death.
The disciples were having a hard time with this.
They could not see him dying
   because they wanted him to be triumphant.
The disciples needed to see things differently.
Jesus is the one who changes blindness to sight.

Last week we heard Jesus ask two of his closest disciples,
   "What is it you want me to do for you?" (Mark 10:36)
They answered,
   "Grant us to sit, one at your right hand and one at your left,
   in your glory." (Mark 10:37)
Their answer showed how out of touch they were with Jesus.
In today's gospel, Jesus asks the same question
   of the blind beggar, Bartimaeus,

"What do you want me to do for you?" (Mark 10:51)
Bartimaeus answered,
    "Master let me see again." (Mark 10:51)
Beggars can't be choosers.
They have to ask for what they really need.
This story abounds in meaning.
The disciples are more blind than the beggar.
They prayed out of greed;
    he prayed out of need.
And what about you? How do you pray?
If Jesus asked you today,
    "What do you want me to do for you?"
    how would you answer?
What do you need?

Before we think of an answer to that question,
    we must consider the kind of society
    in which we ask our questions and dream our dreams.
It's a society dominated by marketing strategies
    out to convince us that we need a lot.
It's a society where twenty-seven percent of prime-time television
    is advertisements that tell you:
    your hair is too curly, or too straight,
    your skin is to light, or too dark,
    your breath and underarms need a spray of mist,
    you are overweight, you are underweight,
    you have zits!
Children, you are led to believe that you will be deprived
    unless you get the newest, latest gadget, gizmo, or toy for Christmas.

What do we really need?
What is it that you want Jesus to do for you?
Why do you come to church?
What is it that you expect from God?
What is it you want for our world, our church, our kids, our future?
If only we could learn to pray
    both as individuals and as a community,

not from our greed but from our need.
We could become like Bartimaeus:
    people who are not afraid of what the crowd thinks and says,
    people who can call on God in tender terms like Bartimaeus did.

And then comes the significant ending.
    Jesus restores sight to Bartimaeus.
And since in the Middle East a favor received is a favor owed,
    Bartimaeus now follows Jesus.
Jesus said, "Go; your faith has made you well." (Mark 10:52)
Whatever his way was before, now it is different.
"Immediately he regained his sight
    and followed him on the way." (Mark 10:52)

This is our story, or should be.
We need to know that when he cures our blindness,
    we'll see him more clearly as the Christ to be followed.
Be careful about what you will be asking for
    because we are saying that we will bear witness with our lives,
    that we share with Jesus his vision of the kingdom of God,
    and that we will do all in our power to bring it about.
To physically open the eyes of the blind as Jesus did for Bartimaeus
    may be beyond us, but we can all take part in bringing
    "new vision" to those who struggle in the darkness.

Let me end with a medieval story.
There were two pilgrims who wanted to go to a shrine
    where they hoped to be made whole
    by bathing in the miraculous waters.
One was blind, and could not see the way.
The other was crippled and could not walk alone.
So they went together, the blind man holding up the cripple
    and the lame man using his eyes to keep them both on the road.
What happened?
Together they reached the healing waters.
And they wound up dancing.

Deut 6:2–6; Heb 7:23–28; Mk 12:28b–34

Give Us A Bumper Sticker, Jesus

"You shall love the Lord your God
with all your heart, and with all your soul,
and with all your mind, and with all your strength." (Mark 12:30)

In an election year,
     particularly in the last weeks and days before voting,
     political candidates attempt to reduce their message
          to sound bites and bumper stickers.
And the truth is, we tend to remember catchy phrases
     more than complex ideas anyway.
It takes great skill to make such a reduction
     in a way that does not sacrifice the truth.
But it was this very request for simplification that confronted Jesus
     when a teacher of the law asked him the question
          contained in today's gospel lesson.
"Which commandment is the first of all?" (Mark 12:28)
The scribe wanted what we all want.
He knew the Old Testament
     contained over seven hundred commands,
     and he wanted to hasten to the bottom line.
He was saying,
"Give us a bumper sticker slogan, Jesus!"

And to his amazement, and perhaps ours as well,
     Jesus does just that.
But in the process, Jesus gives us more than we asked for, too.

Jesus answered simply that you must
    love God with all that you are
    and love your neighbor as yourself.
It was actually not one but two commandments tied together.
The first was from Deuteronomy and the second from Leviticus.
But what's really important is that he called them
    the one commandment.
Together they form the cross of love's command.
Love deep, all the way up to God
    and love wide, all the way to your neighbor.
Deep and wide.
We cannot choose to love God but be unconcerned for humankind.
And we cannot choose to be involved with social issues
    and substitute that concern for a devotion to God.
A follower of God cannot separate the two.
We love deep and wide or our love is crippled.

The late Charles Schulz had a wonderfully subtle way
    of sneaking profound insights into the apparently simple statements
        of his youthful cartoon characters.
For example, Charlie Brown's friend Linus once made the mistake
    of confessing to his sister Lucy
    that he wanted to be a doctor when he grew up.
Lucy was surprised to hear this
    and she responded in her typical, acid-tongued fashion:
    "You, a doctor? That's a laugh! You could never be a doctor!
    You know why? Because you don't love humankind!"
Linus thought about this devastating critique for a moment
    and responded. "I do too love humankind!
        It's people I can't stand!"
Poor Linus, he hadn't embraced that he must love his neighbor as himself.

Love is a strange command.
Other commandments and rules are precise.
We know what it means to steal, to lie, and to kill.
But love is open-ended.

Loving God and loving others can make endless demands
　　but as we grow in one, we grow in the other.
Love can't be put into rules,
　　but images of love can guide us
　　　　and help us understand the ways of God's love.
Let's ponder some of the images of love from Jesus' life:
　　Jesus' loving response to his mother at the wedding feast at Cana;
　　Jesus blessing the children;
　　Jesus touching and healing the sick throughout his ministry;
　　his anger at the money changers in the Temple;
　　his agonized prayer in the garden;
　　his cry of abandonment on the cross.
Each of us has the capacity to love as well as Jesus did.
We have experienced receiving and giving love in our own lives.
When we do, we are loving God as well.

Now, here's a question for you.
Has what you have heard surprised you in any way?
Or have you become indifferent to all this talk
　　of loving God and loving your neighbor?

There are times when it is easy to be
　　cynical and indifferent to the talk of love.
Maybe you and I need to be surprised again
　　into learning that in the kingdom,
　　　　as in life experience,
　　where love is, God is there as well.
I believe that in our effort,
　　our struggle with the mystery of love and being loved,
Jesus may be saying to us today,
　　as he said to the scribe at the end of this gospel reading,
　　"You are not far from the kingdom of God." (Mark 12:34)
Perhaps by the Word we share and the Bread we break,
　　we will draw closer, nearer even than the scribe in today's gospel,
　　　　to the kingdom of God.

1 Kgs 17:10–16; Heb 9:24–28; Mk 12:38–44

Jesus, the People Watcher

For all of them have contributed out of their abundance;
  but she out of her poverty has put in everything she had,
  all she had to live on. (Mark 12:44)

At one time, families would sit around the dining room table
  on Saturday nights discussing how much they could afford
  to put in the contribution envelope
    for the next day's offertory collection.
You may remember this from your own past.
In many parishes the contribution total of each family and individual
  was published annually and distributed for all to scrutinize.
To avoid such public notice, some families gave
  even when it meant something else had to go by the wayside.
These families were victims of that system.
There is something similar in today's gospel.
The poor widow gave the religious institution
  "everything she had, all she had to live on." (Mark 12:44)
She is a victim.
The authorities have nailed the innocent woman to a cross
  in the name of religion.
Her conscience had been shaped to such a fine point
  that she is compelled to hand over almost everything
    of the little she had.

This widow is the patron saint of all such victims
  down through history.
Emotional blackmail under the guise of religion
  allows some television evangelists to make most of their millions
  not from the wealthy, but from the poor.

Usually they are alone and disregarded,
    and the giving can seem a way to be acceptable at least to God,
    even if it is irresponsible giving.

We do not know the widow's name
    and know nothing of her appearance,
    but Jesus is both praising her and pitying her.
As a victim, she has his pity; as a giver, she earns his praise.
And she does maintain her integrity by obeying the law of charity.
There is a well-known saying that
    it's not the gift but the thought that counts.
This truth is easy to document and hard to dispute.
Yet this principle, like many others, can be distorted.
It can be an excuse to justify a miserly attitude toward money.
Since the more important thing
    is the thought behind the gift and not the gift itself,
    then it doesn't really matter how much or how little I give.
I can give a lot or I can give a little,
    but as long as I do it in the right spirit,
    then God must surely be pleased with my stewardship.
Not necessarily so!

Our gospel reading today would certainly seem to teach otherwise.
On this occasion, at the temple,
    Jesus deliberately took a seat in full view of the collection box
    and watched the people as they dropped in their money.
When the service was ended, he pointed out one woman
    and said to his disciples,
    "Truly I tell you, this poor widow has put in more
    than all those who are contributing to the treasury." (Mark 12:43)
This statement has to mean
    that Jesus took note of how much each gave.
Not only did he observe the attitude of their hearts,
    but he also measured the amount of their gifts.
How else could he have known
    which among them had given the most?

Nowadays a good number of pastors do not want to know
    how much individual members contribute to the church.
They don't want to be influenced by the giving habits of the people,
    but want to treat all alike—the large contributor,
        the small contributor, and the non-contributor.
This is a commendable purpose,
    but obviously, Jesus felt no such reluctance.
He deliberately sat and watched how much each person gave.
He was conducting an unannounced competition,
    and when it was over, he declared a winner.
"This poor widow has put in more
    than all those who are contributing to the treasury." (Mark 12 43)

I take this to mean that the Lord measures our giving as well.
If he watched how the Jews gave in the temple,
    surely he watches how his disciples give in the churches.
He is here every Sunday sitting in clear view of the collection box,
    observing the giving habits of his people.
He knows who gives the most.
He knows who gives the least.
He measures our giving,
    but obviously he doesn't go about it in the usual fashion.
If he had, the woman in our story would have finished dead last.

To you and me, it seems like a strange kind of bookkeeping,
    but by his standards it was logical.
He explains it in the last verse of the reading.
"For all of them have contributed out of their abundance,
    but she out of her poverty has put in everything she had,
    all she had to live on." (Mark 12:44)
In other words our gifts are measured not according to size,
    but according to sacrifice.
And that puts things in a totally different light.
Sacrifice to us in a familiar word, but an unfamiliar experience.
How often have we gone without
    in order to give to Christ or the Church?

I'm not asking you to answer the question for me.
And there is no need to answer it for God,
  because God already knows.
But you need to answer it for yourself.
Your giving is an expression of your commitment
  to Christ and the Church.
So it is important what it says to Christ about yourself.

When we give a gift, we take great care to remove the price tag,
  but when we bring our gifts to God, we can't do that.
There is no way to conceal the cost from God.
God measures them, every one,
  and it could be that here today,
  the one who gives the least in terms of money,
    gave the most in terms of love.

Dan 12:1–3; Heb 10:11–14, 18; Mk 13:24–32

This Is Our Hope

"But about that day or hour no one knows,
neither the angels in heaven, nor the Son, but only the Father." (Mark 13:32)

A Japanese airliner crashed and 520 people perished.
In the debris, the search group found a pocket calendar
    of a Japanese businessman with hastily written notes.
"We're not going to make it; I'm sad."
To his family he wrote:
    "To think that our dinner last night
    was the last time we would be together."
To his three children he wrote:
    "Be good, work hard, and help your mother."
The end came suddenly like a thief in the night.

The point of Jesus' remarks today is the same.
None of us knows when the end of our life,
    or all of life on earth, will come.
Therefore, we must be prepared always.
We accept that, in a general sort of way,
    but it really doesn't bother us.
Our concerns are more immediate.
Somebody once said that for every person
    who is worried about the end of the world,
    there must be at least 10,000 who aren't.
This is probably accurate.
The challenge facing most of us is how to deal with life
    as it is, right now, today.

What then, do these end-time Scripture readings
    have to do with people like us?

We don't have to dig very deep before we find all kinds of people
    whose hearts are devoid of hope.
How may people do you know
    who look to tomorrow with hope and expectancy?
Cynicism has become a symbol for the mood of the day.
Optimism is regarded as something reserved for
    those too blind to see or too weak to handle the realities of life.

There was a cartoon about four golfers on the eighteenth green, about to finish.
In the background was a skyline of a city, and above it,
    a mushroom cloud caused by an atomic explosion.
Underneath was the caption,
    "Go ahead and putt.
    The shock waves won't hit us for a least thirty seconds."
Our world, our country are full of troubled uncertainties.
In the midst of this doubt and insecurity the truth is clear.
If you and I are to face the future with anything akin to hope,
    we must find that hope within it.
This is today's gospel theme.

There are those who believe that the words of today's gospel
    refer specifically and exclusively
    to the time we are now living in.
But remember, Jesus told his disciples that their generation
    would not pass away until all these things would be fulfilled.
The truth is that no generation passes away
    without the fulfillment of these things.
We live in that kind of world.
Jesus told his disciples 2000 years ago and he is telling us today:
Expect trouble.
Do not be surprised by it or resentful of it; it is a part of living.
He also indicated that the midst of that trouble is where
    we most clearly see his "great power and glory."
That is the lesson we desperately need to learn.
Far too often our outlook on life is nothing
    but a reaction to current events.
If things look good, we are hopeful.

If things go badly, we lose heart.
We are like weather vanes, changing with every shift of the wind.
We are optimistic today, and pessimistic tomorrow.
That kind of shifting hope is not worth very much.

What we really need is to wrap our minds around something solid,
    and hold on to that through the fair and foul weather.
Jesus faced the future with hope,
      because he had something solid to hold on to:
          the eternal truth of God that can never pass away.
You see, real hope is never just a happy mood,
      borrowed from fortunate circumstances.
Real hope, genuine hope, lasting hope
    is the outgrowth of faith.
If a person believes, as Jesus did
    that this is God's world and the final say belongs to him,
    then the future is hopeful.

However troubled the present may be,
    life has a beginning, a middle, and an end.
It has a goal, a purpose, and a conclusion.
In other words, it will make sense.
Our lives are novels we write while living them.
Our lives are journeys with succeeding stages.
We dare not get stuck in youthful crises,
      middle-age malaise, or senior self-pity.
We have a goal, a finish line, and a place to go.
It doesn't matter when life ends,
    whether it ends in the middle of a war
    or at the consecration of the Mass.
All that matters is that we are part of the drama Jesus describes.
So do not let the world pass you by on its way to the end.
    "Heaven and earth will pass away,
    but my words will not pass away." (Mark 13:31)
Nor will those who believe it
    and whose lives are shaped by that faith pass away.

Dan 7:13–14; Rev 1:5–8; Jn 18:33b–37

He Never Sought the Title

"My kingdom is not from this world." (John 18:36)
"I came into the world to testify to the truth." (John 18:37)
"Everyone who belongs to the truth listens to my voice." (John 18:37)

> He prayed; it wasn't my religion.
> He ate; it wasn't what I ate.
> He spoke; it wasn't my language.
> He dressed; it wasn't what I wore.
> He took my hand; it wasn't the color of mine.
> But when he laughed, it was how I laughed
> And when he cried, it was how I cried.
>
> —Amy Maddox, sixteen years old

The United States of America came into existence
   by throwing out the king of England.
In spite of our anti-royal origins,
   we have a fascination with royalty, particularly English royalty.
We speculate whether Charles or William will succeed Elizabeth.
We are glued to the TV for a royal wedding or funeral.
Jesus Christ is a king. But he wasn't crowned in Westminster Abbey.
His kingdom is not of this world,
   but it doesn't mean that it is not in this world.
This makes Jesus more fascinating than any earthly king or queen.
Here is a little test.
  What king married Isabella and sent an Italian
  to sail the ocean blue?
    Answer: Ferdinand.
  What king was not happy with the Catholic Church
  and had his wife beheaded?
    Answer: Henry XIII.

What king loved his blue suede shoes?
  Answer: Elvis Presley.
What good king looked out when the snow lay 'round about,
deep, and crisp and even?
  Answer: Good King Wensceslas.
What king called for three fiddlers, a pipe, and a bowl?
  Answer: Old King Cole.
Who was the large, hairy king
who fought off airplanes in New York City?
  Answer: King Kong.

See, in spite of living in a nation that values democracy,
    and finds the notion of kingship rather odd,
    we know quite a bit on this subject.
Finally, who was the man who never sought the title,
    but was called the King of the Jews?
The answer is in today's gospel: Jesus.

What is the kingdom of God like?
Is it a kingdom of justice, love, peace, and life?
The kingdom of God is found in places that, for most of us,
    are not the easiest or most comfortable places to be.
Think about today's gospel for a moment.
Jesus stands alone before Pilate, rejected by the crowd,
    condemned by the chief priests and Sanhedrin.
At that moment he is counted among
    the powerless, the voiceless, the vulnerable, those on the margins.
And still he is present where human need is greatest.
Before Pilate he declares,
"For this I came into the world, to testify to the truth." (John 18:37)

The values that govern his kingdom
    are seen in the lives of those who respond from the heart
    to the needs of the poor, the powerless, the vulnerable,
    and those on the margins.
What his kingdom is like is glimpsed in the lives of those who,
    without giving it much thought, reach out to someone in need.

It may be family, neighbor, friend, or stranger.
No training is required for this.
No academic qualifications are necessary.
No knighthood.
All it takes is an eye to notice, a heart to respond, and a will to act,
    no matter how small the action may seem.

So if you seek the kingdom of God, look around you
    and be ready to stand by and with him.
Christ our King, we thank you
    for ending this last Sunday of the Church year on a note of hope.
In all things, and in our own day, Christ, our King,
    may your kingdom come, and may your will be done.

A Glimpse of Fr. Hayes

I saw Fr. Hayes weep only two times, and each time the assembly wept with him. One was when he announced, at his forty-year jubilee celebration, the death of the beloved world-class tenor, Frank Patterson. Only a few months before, Frank Patterson had performed in Holy Angels Church.

The next time he cried was when he revealed at a Saturday evening Mass in June 2003, that his left lung had collapsed as a result of cancer. He had to take the summer off to be treated for this major health problem. But he still managed to continue to crack jokes. At his last Mass at Holy Angels announcing his retirement, he mentioned that he had consulted with his earthly boss, the bishop of the Diocese of Duluth. He told him that he had played a round of golf with the young undertaker in the small town of Moose Lake. In spite of his health difficulties, he beat him.

The bishop replied, "Well, if you are going to beat someone in golf, the undertaker is a good man to beat!" In addition, the bishop had given Fr. Mike permission to sit down during the Mass. To which the small-town cleric replied, "If you have seen the pope lately, you will notice that sometimes during the Mass, he sits when he should be standing. Now," said Fr. Hayes, "I'm in the same league as the pope."

His optimism continued through the summer of his final illness. I was amazed that he continued to play golf with his friends…and I even heard he was giving putting advice to a novice golfer toward the end of his days. He did not dote or mentally labor over his illness.

    — Dr. John Connolly, Cloquet, MN

Other Feasts
& Occasions

Rev 7:2–3, 9–14; 1 Jn 3:1–3; Mt 5:1–12a

Wheel of Fortune

Tonight I watched "Wheel of Fortune" with the sound turned down,
  and it's not the same show.
Try it sometime yourself.
What you'll miss is not so much Pat Sajak's snappy comments,
  Vanna White, of course, who says very little,
  or the contestant's responses
    (who are usually just mentioning a consonant, or a vowel).
Without the sound track, what's really missing is the audience.
It's strange, but you never see the audience in that show.
But you hear them cheering their favorites on,
  sharing in the ecstasy of their victory, or
  moaning with them in the agony of defeat.
You may be wondering where all this is heading.

The "Wheel of Fortune" audience is a bit like the crowd of saints
  whose feast we celebrate today.
Like that audience, the saints are there,
  just out of sight and cheering us on through life.
Like turning the sound down on "Wheel of Fortune,"
  we, too, have turned the sound down.
We don't hear the saints anymore, and it is just not the same show.
It is difficult to explain why this has happened.
After all, sanctity is what we are all about as Church.
It is our reason for existence, to make saints of each other.
You'd think we would appreciate the constant reminder
  that those who have gone before us
  found sanctity not only possible, but enjoyable.
How do we change the situation?

We don't have to go far.

We already feast with them at this Eucharistic table.

But like the audience we don't see on the show,
    they are present and cheering us on.

They're already here.

Turn the sound up and listen to what they have to say.

Dan 12:1–3; 1 Cor 15:51–57; Jn 5:24–29

The Dead

When we love someone we don't want them to die.
Life has intrinsic value.
The Welsh poet, Dylan Thomas,
    expresses this sentiment in the famous words
        addressed to his dying father.
    Do not go gentle into that good night,
    Old age should burn and rage at the close of day:
    Rage, rage against the dying of the light.
This is firmly in the spirit of Christ's resurrection,
    which affirms our natural desire for life, and life alone.

We Christians are not to deny the fact of death
    anymore than we can deny the fact of sin.
But both are unwanted interlopers in our lives.
We acknowledge the reality of death without affirming its goodness. Yet every
time we celebrate the liturgy,
    we commemorate Jesus' own death.
His death conquered all death.
He transformed all death back into life.

A variety of different popular customs
    are associated with All Souls Day.
Of particular interest is El Dia de los Muertos (The Day of the Dead),
    celebrated throughout Mexico.
November 2 is celebrated more elaborately in Mexico
    than other places.
In preparation for the day
    (actually it is a two-day celebration, November 1-2),
    altars are erected in homes, schools,
        or on the tombs of the deceased.

They are lavishly decorated with flowers,
    especially marigolds.
Fruits, dozens of candles, and the favorite foods of the deceased
    are placed on and around the altar.
Children's graves are strewn with toys and candies.
Cakes, cookies, and special breads shaped like skulls or mummies
    are baked for the occasion.

Children often dress in costumes with masks
    and carry pumpkin lanterns through the streets
        in midnight processions to the cemeteries.
The are accompanied by tolling bells
    and many will spend the entire night at the graveside,
        praying, singing, eating, and reminiscing.
While these customs may seem unusual
    for those unfamiliar with them,
    they do seem to affirm the communion
    that exists among the faithful on both sides of death.

In the Apostle's Creed, we profess,
    "We believe in the communion of saints."
So what is All Souls Day all about?
First, we ask to be blessed
    with the memories of loved ones who have died.
To remember those who have died is to honor them.

In the fable "The Old House,"
    Hans Christian Anderson tells the story of a little boy
    who befriends an old man living alone in an old house.
One day he gives the man one of his cherished toy tin soldiers.
But the tin soldier becomes very unhappy
    and asks the boy to return him to the boy's house,
        which is full of life.
The boy, however, is convinced that the old man's house is full of life,
    in as much as it is full of wonderful memories.
He explains this to the toy soldier, who refuses to hear.

And so the soldier leaps off his shelf
and falls through the floor boards of the old house
onto the ground below.
Many years later, long after the old man has died
and the house is torn down,
the boy, now a young man,
finds the tin soldier half-buried in the dirt.
Nearby they discover a faded piece of leather
that had once been emblazoned with paint,
and had hung on the walls of the old man's house.
The boy is again flooded with warm memories of the old man.
He realizes that memories, like this old piece of leather,
lose their brightness and color,
but always keep their fabric and texture.
But he cannot convince the tin soldier of this.
The fabric and texture of the memories of those who have died
should console us.

Today, we also pray to deepen our appreciation for the gift of life.
Life is like the wind.
We do not know exactly where it comes from
or where it is to go.
We do not know how or why it continues at any given moment.
We are supported by a power beyond ourselves:
God's love.
When we reflect on death, we can reflect on our resolve
to live life to the fullest.
Many say, after all,
that this is precisely what the dead would want of us.
We need to nourish more deeply
the spark that illuminates each moment of our living and hoping.
To celebrate and honor all souls in today's feast,
we need to commit ourselves to life.
Life in all of its beginnings, middles, and endings.

We need to develop a holy hatred for all forms of death,
especially those of war, executions, abortion, and euthanasia.

Albert Camus, a French philosopher, said before he died,
    "There will be no lasting peace,
        either in the heart of individuals or in social customs,
        until death is outlawed."

Respect for life honors those who have died
    and gives strength to us left behind.
All Souls Day becomes the time for finishing grief work,
    for affirming the communion of saints,
        and for celebrating a victory over death and darkness
            through memory, story, and hope.

Ezek 47:1–2, 8–9, 12; 1 Cor 3:9c–11, 16–17; Jn 2:13–22

Mother of All Churches

Today's feast celebrates the dedication of a church
  with a very odd title.
There is no saint by the name of John Lateran.
The lateran was a complex of buildings,
    built on land owned by the Lateran family,
    and given to the pope by the Emperor Constantine
      in the fourth century.
The church was first called the Most Holy Savior.
Later the church was renamed for St. John the Baptist.
This church, not St. Peter's, is the cathedral of the bishop of Rome.
So it is considered the mother of all churches throughout the world.

That is why we celebrate this feast as a solemnity.
It is a celebration of our unity
    with Catholic churches around the world.
It is a celebration of our unity with the bishop of Rome, the Pope.
In the context of our November focus on All Saints and All Souls,
    this feast reminds us of the third part of the communion of saints:
      the Church on earth.

We celebrate who we are as the people of God called "Church."
In the resort town of Huntington Beach in southern California
    there are two singularly different churches.
Both are Catholic.
One is traditional, the other contemporary.
At the traditional church, the Mass is celebrated in Latin;
    communion is received on the tongue; and
    such ancient hymns as "O Sanctisima" break the hushed silence.
There is no Sign of Peace.

On the other side of town,
    a contemporary Mass is being celebrated in English;
    young people tune their guitars encouraging
    the congregation to join them in singing of a new song of praise. Altar girls
walk freely around the sanctuary
    and lay people assist the celebrant
    in the distribution of communion in the hand.
The Sign of Peace is an exuberant event
    as people greet each other with a handshake, a word, a hug.

Each of these eucharistic celebrations are Catholic,
    and we the Church must continue to hold such diversity
    without splitting apart, or be torn by dissension.
As one spiritual writer so wisely wrote,
    in essentials unity,
    in non-essentials freedom, in all things charity."

The dioceses of Lincoln, Nebraska and Saginaw, Michigan
    are textbook examples of diversity.
The most interesting contrast between the two dioceses
    may be in their celebration of the liturgy.
Lincoln's liturgical strategy was to distance the priest
    from the congregation,
    stressing the sacral rather than the communal.
For Saginaw, the effort was to reduce the distance
    between priest and people,
    and to stress the communal meal aspect of the Eucharist.
In both dioceses parishioners receive communion quite differently;
    in both, they attend Mass in about the same percentages,
        which is somewhat above the national average.
In many ways they give us a picture of American Catholicism
    as we begin the twenty-first century.

Where would Jesus go to church,
    to one that's traditional or one that's contemporary?
We might take a hint from the gospel story concerning Zacchaeus:
    "He has gone to be the guest of one who is a sinner." (Luke 19:7)

Jesus could have stayed with anyone he chose.
Zacchaeus was not your garden variety sinner.
He was a turncoat, a traitor, and a thief—big time!
Why did Jesus go home with a man like that?
My guess is it was because he felt welcome.
Zacchaeus was a sinner all right, but he knew it, no bones about it,
    and Christ will always feel welcome with people like that.

In the second reading, St. Paul speaks of the Church when he tells us
    "You are God's building, the Spirit dwelling within you."
The foundation that he laid for each one of us and for the Church
    is the foundation of charity.
"Love one another as I have loved you." (John 15:12)
At this liturgy, as we celebrate the building of the Church,
    let us pray that despite our differences we may find
    unity in the essentials, strength in our differences,
        and charity in all things.

In this new millennium,
    fortified with a deep love for the Church,
    let us pray with confidence today's psalm
    "God is within, it cannot be shaken.
    God will help it at the dawning of the day." (Psalm 46:6)

A Glimpse of Fr. Hayes

Upon occasion, I would talk to Fr. Mike about church and theological matters. Sometime after the death of Mother Teresa, I read that the rites of exorcism were read over her as she lay on her deathbed. Fr. Mike's take on that situation I found to be very interesting.

* "Ah John," he offered, "the devil doesn't care too much about little fish like you and me. What he is after are the heavy hitters like Mother Teresa."*

*   — Dr. John Connolly, Cloquet, MN*

Num 21:4b–9; Phil 2:6–11; Jn 3:13–17

The Triumph of Failure

The first reading from the Book of Numbers
    probably brings about some head shaking or puzzlement.
It should.
Who believes in a God who presumably sends
    a horde of poisonous snakes to punish his people?
This is from the Hebrew Scriptures,
    but how many times have Christians been told of a God
    who threatened people with eternal fire for a single misdeed,
        like missing a Mass on Sunday?
We need to sort this out.

The episode in Numbers is one tribe's idea of God—
    a very bad one, at that.
The same Hebrew Scriptures eventually portray God as
    slow to anger, full of compassion, ever ready to relent.
They even call him a saving God, a merciful God.

In the gospel today, Jesus is talking not of hellfire,
    but of eternal life.
The gospel says that
    "so must the Son of Man be lifted up." (John 3:14)
What does this mean?
We rightly think of the cross, but it has a second meaning:
    the resurrection and exaltation of Jesus to,
    as the gospel puts it, "the right hand of God."
The cross is everywhere in Christian life:
    in our churches, in our art, traced upon ourselves.
Protestant Christians favor the cross without the body
    as a reminder that "He is risen; he is not here."
Roman Catholics and Orthodox Christians

favor the image of the Crucified One, perhaps to say
   he is still here, sharing the pain of the world,
   the passion endured by so many.

The cross is the most widely recognized sign of Christianity.
It is with this sign we bless ourselves, others, and various objects.
No other major religion has such a puzzling,
   even contradictory, symbol as its logo,
      its insignia or banner.
Once the cross was one of the world's most hated signs,
   similar to the electric chair, gas chamber, guillotine,
   firing squad, hanging rope, or lethal injection.
What originally was a sign of punishment and death
   is now a symbol of abundant life.
Our Mass has as its theme the Triumph of the Cross.
When the early Christians first began to honor the cross
   because of its close association with Jesus,
St. Paul called it an obstacle to the Jews
   and madness to the Greeks and Romans.

Death by crucifixion was officially terminated about 350 AD,
   but the crosses have continued to multiply.
It is still a sign of pain, but the pain it represents
   is the price of victory and salvation.
As the water falling generates electricity,
   God transforms our efforts into light and heat.
As the sea transforms rock to sand,
   God transforms our weakness into strength.
It is a little strange that we call today's feast
   "the Triumph of the Cross,"
   for "triumph" has overtones of winning and conquering.

This is not the mystery of the cross.
The cross is about life and love.
But triumph does remind us that Jesus broke through death to life,
   that against the odds, good prevails.

Thinking clearly about the mystery of the cross
 leads us to think of God differently,
  and this leads us to different ways of thinking of others.

God deals with us in love, especially in times of difficulty and trouble.
God is not the source of our troubles.
We can blame all our troubles on the devil, the fall of Adam,
 or a God who is powerless in a random universe.
God is with us in our pain.
God is with us even in death.
God enables us to endure, break through to life, even beyond death.
Because God is a God not of violence, but of love,
 our dealings with each other need to be of love, not of violence.
This is the work of a lifetime.
It's easier to compete, put down, violate truth, criticize, be aggressive,
 and punish; but God and goodness are not in violence.
We find our humanity when we strive
 to accept, protect, endure, and forgive.
The triumph of Jesus' cross becomes the triumph of our crosses, too.

Nurse Sheila Cassidy was jailed and tortured in Chile
 as a prisoner of conscience several years ago.
Out of that experience she wrote the following victory poem
 found in her book, *Sharing the Darkness*:

 I believe,
  no pain is lost.
 No tear unmarked,
  no cry of anguish
  dies unheard,
  lost in a hail of gunfire
  or blanked out by the padded cell.
 I believe that pain
  and prayer are somehow saved,
  processed,
  stored,
  used in the Divine Economy.

The blood
    shed in Salvador
    will irrigate the heart
    of some financier
    a million miles away.
The terror,
    pain,
    despair,
    swamped
    by lava, flood, or earthquake,
    will be caught up like mist and fall again,
    a gentle rain on arid hearts
    or souls despairing
    in the back streets
    of Brooklyn.

We celebrate this Eucharist in memory of Christ
    who died on the cross and who rose to life.
Let's pray for faith that believes in the Triumph of the Cross.

Gen 3:9–15, 20; Eph 1:3–6, 11–12; Lk 11:27–28

A Big Difference

A shoeshine boy was plying his trade
    outside Grand Central Station in New York City.
A silver medal danced at his neck
    as he slapped his shine cloth, again and again,
    across the shoes of a man.
After watching the medal for a while,
    the man said curiously,
"Sonny, what's that hardware around your neck?"
"It's a medal of the mother of Jesus," the boy said.
"But why her medal?" asked the man.
    "She's no different from your mother."
"You could be right," said the boy,
    "but there sure is a big difference between her son and me."
The man knocked the ashes from his cigar,
    slapped a dollar in the boy's hand, and walked off.

The boy's answer was not only good diplomacy,
    but also good theology.
Both are sometimes needed
    when talking to non-Catholics about Mary.
But this was not always the case.

The poet William Wordsworth,
    once called Mary
        "Our tainted nature's solitary boast."
Wordsworth's beautiful phrase explains why Catholics
    celebrate the feast of the Immaculate Conception.
It is because Mary is indeed
        "Our tainted nature's solitary boast."
She alone was preserved without sin.

The mother of God is periodically presented to us for reflection
    not because of her differences from us
    but surprisingly, because of her similarities with us.
This is a woman who knew many of the same trials and doubts as we,
    perhaps even more.
Hers was a heart stabbed with
    suffering,
    lack of understanding,
    a sense of failure,
    silent rejection,
    and non-comprehension of the ways and means of her child.
It was certainly no easier for her to maintain faith and hope
    than it is for us to do.
After all, her trials preached the resurrection.

It is just when all appears lost,
    when the adolescent heart is broken for the first time,
    when the middle-aged man or woman questions life,
    when one has suffered the unspeakable loss of a child, and
    when our past dilemma presents no way out.
It is just here that we stand with this magnificent woman
    at the foot of the cross.
Perhaps she offers no more solutions than we do
    to suffering and loneliness.
She offers, however, her presence that is caring and constant.
This is the woman who is of us and for us.

God invites you today to better know this woman, Mary;
    perhaps today God introduces you
        to this woman for the first time.
Do not let the day pass
    without coming to know her a little better
    than so many of us did when she was only
        "Hail Mary, full of grace," to us.
She was undefiled,
    therefore, so unlike ourselves, who need each other so much.
The feast of the Immaculate Conception is for us.

This is the feast of the beauty of God in a mother's heart.
This is the feast of the power of grace in a woman's heart.
May Our Lady help us to purify ourselves
    so that we may be able to travel with her
        toward the crib of Jesus.
Let us look into our own hearts
    and close with a prayer taken from Carey Landry's hymn
    "Hail Mary, Gentle Woman."

>Gentle woman,
>peaceful dove,
>Teach us wisdom,
>teach us love.

A Wedding Homily

This afternoon we are celebrating the wedding
 of Mary Colleen and Robert.
It is the hour that makes the beginning of marriage,
 a lifetime together.
We wish you well as you face the challenge of building
 a beautiful life together.
As friends and relatives, we bring you our gifts and our support,
 not just by wedding presents,
 but with gifts of understanding and prayer.
We pray that we can offer you the ultimate wedding gift,
 something in our own lives that you can imitate,
 something that inspires and encourages you.

You are beginning the journey of a lifetime
 and this wedding is the point of departure.
We celebrate with you as you begin this journey because you travel
 with a capacity for joy and love,
 an openness to new thoughts,
 an eye for beauty,
 and a readiness for new adventure.
The freedom of such a journey sets our blood tingling.

As we celebrate the marriage of Mary Colleen and Robert,
 this liturgy is a kind of farewell (or fare-thee-well) celebration
 for two young travelers who are setting out
 on a new and exciting journey together, to discover
 new aspects of self and each other,
 new beauties, new love,
 new difficulties, and new challenges.
We want to wish you bon voyage and Godspeed.

We suggest that you don't take too much heavy old baggage with you,
    which will impede your freedom to move.
May you fly on the wings of God as you shape your future together.
This is important; your marriage is your own unique journey.
You may know of others who have set out with enthusiasm
    on a similar journey only to end up in shipwreck.
This should not be a source of discouragement.
You are the masters of your marital destiny.
You are not statistics.
You will encounter many challenges and problems,
    but if they are handled together in a spirit of trust,
    they will strengthen the tough fibers of your togetherness.

There is a little poem that affirms our will
    to make choices and determine our destiny:

One ship drives east, and one drives west
With self same winds that blow.
It's the set of the sails, and not the gales,
That tell them where to go.

Like the winds of the sea, are the winds of fate,
As we voyage along through life.
It's the set of the soul that decides its goal,
And not the calm or the strife.

— Ella Wheeler Wilcox, "Winds of Fate"

It is not what happens in your marriage that will make it successful,
    it is how you choose to handle what happens
        that will determine its growth.
You know that already from your experiences
    in your relationship to this point.
So we encourage you to chart a magnificent destiny for yourselves. This is a
vocation, a challenge to you from God,
    and it will bond you together
    in one of the deepest satisfactions of marriage: mutual support.

What is love?
The children on Sesame Street were asked this question
    and they came up with many answers.
But they finally decided that "love is blind."
For all of us, love has a special meaning.
For psychologists, love is letting go of fear.
For religious, love is God and God is Love.
For a child, love is a pool at the Holiday Inn.
The dictionary says that love is attraction based on sexual desire,
    a strong affection, a warm attachment,
    or a score of zero in tennis.
We can all agree with the poet who tells us that
"Love is not love until it is given away."
By giving our love away,
    we increase the love within us and everybody gains.

Today, we celebrate love in your marriage,
    a love which is being given away to each other, forever.
It is our prayer for you that your love
    will continue to grow and deepen throughout the years.
You will create your own uniqueness to the question,
    "What is love?"

We pray that the Holy Spirit will help you create
    your own definition of love.
Then there will be no need for us to have to say,
    "love is Bogart and Bacall."
When we think of love, we want to be immediately reminded that
    "love is Mary and Bob."

—Given for the wedding of
Mary Colleen Groh and Robert Joseph Dado,
June 25, 1986